VIET

Text by
David Tornquist

Originated and developed by
Nebojša Bato Tomašević

NAM

Photographs and captions by
Guido Alberto Rossi

Design by
Gane Aleksić

A Motovun Group Book

© Flint River Press Ltd. 1991

First published in the U.K. in 1991
by FLINT RIVER PRESS Ltd.
26 Litchfield Street, London WC2H 9NJ

Distributed by Philip Wilson Publishers Ltd.
26 Litchfield Street, London WC2H 9NJ

ISBN: 1-871489-08-3

Editor
Madge Phillips

Works of art reproduced by kind permission of
Mr. and Mrs. Gavro Altman of Belgrade
Mr. and Mrs. Herbert von Bank of Bonn

Colour separation by
Summerfield Press, Florence

Printed and bound in Italy by
Zincografica Fiorentina, Florence

CONTENTS

CHRONOLOGY

2878 B.C.	Legendary founding of Van-lang by the first Hung king
830-300 B.C.	Dong Son culture
111 B.C.	Han dynasty extends Chinese dominion over Red River Valley
44 A.D.	Chinese end five-year rule of Trung sisters
249	Revolt led by the Lady Trieu
547	Ly Bon assassinated and his army defeated by Chinese
618-907	Chinese T'ang dynasty
679	Chinese first refer to Vietnam as Annam ('Defeated South')
939	Vietnam gains independence from China
1010-1225	Ly dynasty, country known as Dai Viet
1069	Champa forced to cede three of its northern provinces
1070	Founding of Van Mieu, Temple of Literature, for study of Confucianism
1075	First literary examinations for positions in civil service
1225-1400	Tran dynasty
1257-1287	Three Mongol invasions defeated under leadership of Tran Hung Dao
1371	Invading army from Champa pillages Thang Long (Hanoi)
1400-1408	Reign of innovative Emperor Ho Qui Ly
1408-1427	Vietnam again a province of China
1428	Le Loi frees country and becomes Emperor Le Thai To
1428-1789	Le dynasty titular rulers, but not effective after 1527
1460-1497	Reign of Le Thanh To, entitled Hong Duc ('Great Virtue')
1527-1592	Mac family wields power in Vietnam
1545	Nguyen and Trinh families defeat Mac forces and take control of south
1592	Mac family removed and Trinh takes ascendancy
1620	Nguyen family achieves effective control of southern provinces
1627-1672	Trinh wages war to regain southern provinces from Nguyen
1651	Alexandre de Rhodes, French Jesuit, publishes Vietnamese grammar and dictionary in Rome
1672	Trinh and Nguyen families initiate century of peaceful coexistence
1771	Tay Son Rebellion
1789	Nguyen Hué proclaims himself Emperor Quang Trung
1802-1945	Nguyen dynasty
1802-1820	Reign of Gia Long (Nguyen Anh), adoption of Gia Long Code
1820-1841	Reign of Minh Mang, anti-Western Confucianist
1874	French establish sovereignty over Cochin China
1883	Tonkin and Annam made French protectorates
1887	France forms Indochinese Union
1924	Major find of Bronze-Age culture at Dong Son on Ma River
1925	Nguyen Ai Quoc (Ho Chi Minh) founds Vietnam Revolutionary Youth League
1930	Strike on Michelin rubber plantation at Phu Rieng Indochinese Communist Party formed
1940	Japanese occupy Vietnam
1941	Viet Minh created as national front led by Communists
1945	In March the Japanese replace the French administration Viet Minh proclaims independent republic in August Revolution
1946	In November French gunboat fires on crowd on Haiphong quay Hostilities of First Indochina War begin in December
1954	Battle of Dien Bien Phu on eve of Geneva peace conference Ngo Dinh Diem becomes prime minister of newly formed South Vietnam
1963	Diem and his brother Ngo Dinh Nhu assassinated
1964	'Tonkin Gulf' resolution passed in U.S. Congress
1965	U.S. Marines land near Danang in March
1968	Tet Offensive begins in late January
1969	U.S. troop strength in Vietnam reaches peak of over half a million
1972	Easter Offensive
1973	U.S.A. and North Vietnam sign peace treaty in Paris Last U.S. combat troops withdrawn
1975	Fall of Saigon
1978	U.S.S.R. and Socialist Republic of Vietnam sign 25-year friendship treaty
1979	Vietnam invades Cambodia, replaces Pol Pot regime with its own government China conducts 'punitive' invasion of Vietnam's northern border region
1989	Hanoi announces withdrawal of last Vietnamese troops from Cambodia

1. A peasant already at work in the fields at sunrise. The results of such a hard life are very meager: Vietnam has not been meeting its needs for food. Even rice, the staple of the diet, had to be imported until 1989. ▷

2. Aerial view of the Mekong Delta. The river is 2620 miles in length but flows through Vietnamese territory for only 136 miles. The delta covers are area of 15,500 square miles in the far south of the country. The soil is fertile but less than half the land is cultivated (mainly with rice), because of the lack of a drainage system which would enable the Vietnamese to reclaim the land (much of it below sea level) from the salt marshes. ▷ ▷

3. A branch of the immense Mekong River. It is still the only access route for many delta villages. ▷ ▷ ▷

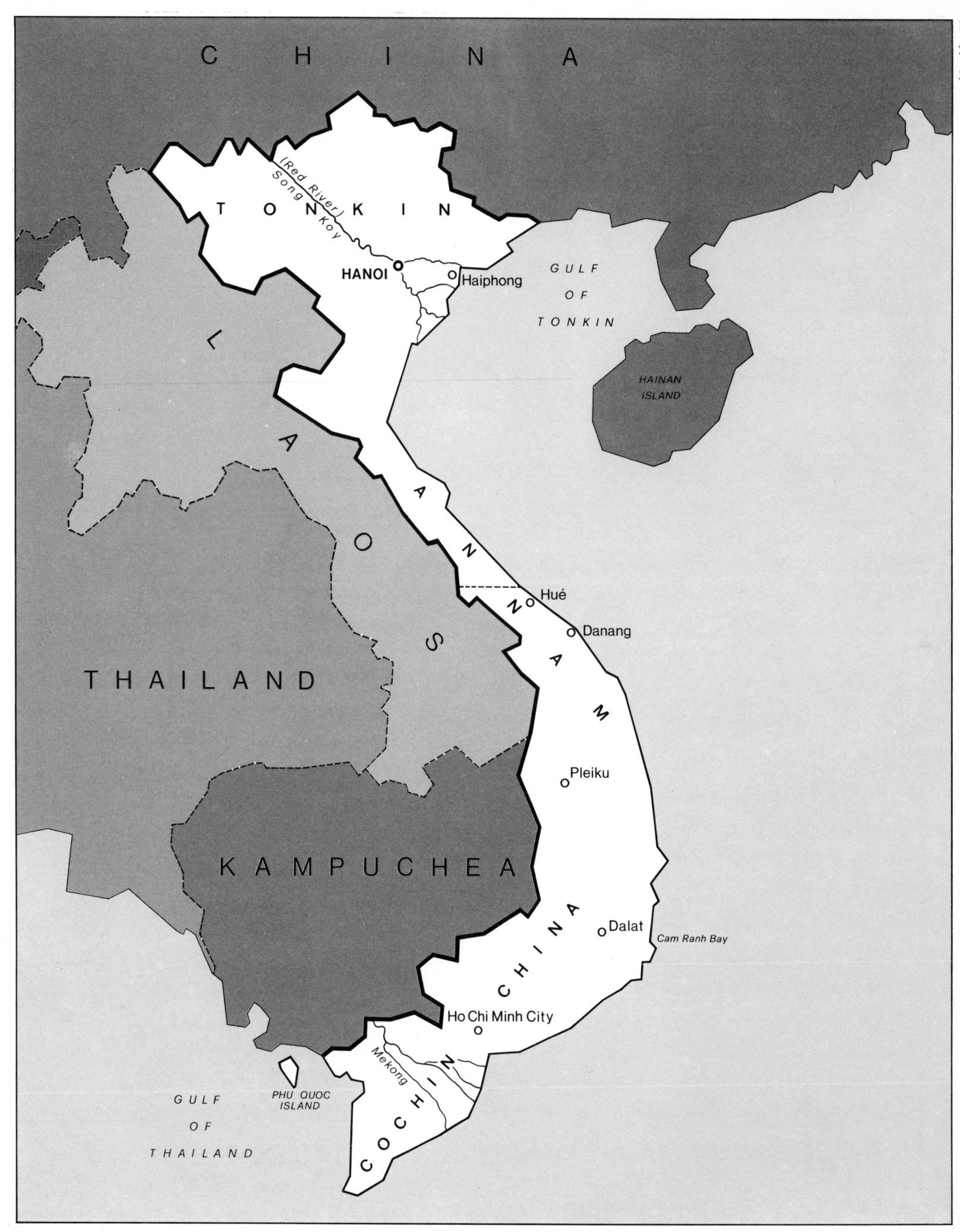

4

4. *Panoramic view of rice fields; bomb craters are still clearly visible 20 years after the war. Although the surface scars are more in evidence, the damage done to the land through the use of toxins is much more serious. Agent Orange, used to defoliate Viet Cong action zones, and absorbed by the soil, appears to be to blame for the increase of malformations in newborn children since the war.*

5

5.   Rice is still cultivated in Vietnam by wading knee-deep in water behind a buffalo-drawn plow. The lack of mechanization makes draft animals invaluable. In wartime, peasants used to hide them in their huts when soldiers were approaching.

6.   Temple in a paddy field by the road leading from Da Nang (Danang) to Hoi Nam, a sign of deeply rooted spirituality in a country which, despite the Communist regime, has remained faithful to its religious heritage. ▷

7.   Ha Long Bay, which opens onto Tonkin Gulf, and its impressive panorama of limestone islands. Local legend sees them as scales on the back of a dragon (water spirit) and a heron (mountain spirit), the two creatures from which the Viet race springs. ▷ ▷

8.   Typical scene on the river near Nha Trang. Fishing villages raised on piles are surrounded by tall coconut palms. The river is always busy with vessels of all shapes and sizes. ▷ ▷ ▷

Land of the Dragon-Fish

PHYSICAL RELIEF

Anyone can see the legendary dragon-fish on a map of Vietnam. Its broad fluted tail represents the country's northern portion, whose axis is the Red River. The twisting body imitates the mountain chain that conforms to the curving shore of the South China Sea, leaving only a narrow coastal strip. And the head, bent westward, suggests the broadened southern region of Vietnam, where plateaus step down in a southwest direction from the mountain range to the lowlands of the Mekong Delta. Still lower lands of the Ca Mau Peninsula make the snout.

People have seen other things. In the early Fifties the French saw De Gaulle with his famous nose pointed toward Singapore. Another fanciful, but meaningful comparison is the image of two baskets of rice suspended at either end of a peasant's bamboo carrying-pole. This one tells us that the northern and southern ends of the country are broad while its central section is slender. It identifies even more aptly the principal sources of the country's food supply — the rice-growing deltas of the Red River in the north and the Mekong in the south — and above all the industrious and resourceful Vietnamese peasant who farms them.

Vietnam is so long and narrow that its water boundary (1563 miles) on the South China Sea and the Gulf of Thailand is only slightly shorter than its land boundary. China is the neighbor to the north and Laos and Cambodia on the west. The length north to south is 1200 miles; the width varies from a maximum of 375 miles in the north to a slim 31 miles in the central portion. The natural border of northern mountains which stood as a boundary of Vietnam even when it was a province of China is no protective barrier. For the thousand years that northern Vietnam was part of China it allowed the Chinese army, administration and settlers ample access and communication. In the thirteenth century Kublai Khan crossed it with an army of no less than half a million men. The border with Laos, however, runs through jungle and forest in high mountains that represent a formidable barrier to east-west travel. The Annamite Cordillera, the backbone of the dragon-fish, rises steeply from the narrow coastal plain on the eastern side and the few passes are not accommodating. Most of the border with Cambodia runs through upland jungle and swampy

9. A diminutive herder with his buffalo, indispensable to the Vietnamese farming household. When the party finally abandoned the rigid agricultural collectivization plan, allowing small-scale private enterprise to develop, life continued to be difficult for the peasant. Unfavorable weather conditions and various plant diseases lower the agricultural output.

lowlands to reach the Gulf of Siam.

Vietnam's area is 128,000 square miles, roughly the size of Norway or Finland or four-fifths the size of California. But the distribution of that land between lowlands amenable to agriculture and travel and the uplands covered with dense forest and jungle is very onesided. The plains take up no more than one-fifth, yet support 90 percent of the country's population of 66 million. The hills and mountains have been inhabited since prehistoric times by a great diversity of small tribal peoples with a primitive pattern of life and farming.

Vietnam's own major regions are as distinct and clearly defined as the parts of the dragon-fish. The Vietnamese refer to them as the northern, central and southern sections (Bac Bo, Trung Bo and Nam Bo). Without implying any reference to French administrative divisions, foreigners find it convenient to use the already familiar names of Tonkin for the north, Annam the central portion, and Cochinchina the south.

TONKIN

Tonkin is the ancient home of the Vietnamese, who have been developing their civilization along the Ma and Red rivers for better than two thousand years of recorded history. If archeological evidence continues to bear out what Vietnamese legend suggests, their ancestry can be traced back another two thousand years through a succession of cultures in this area.

Tonkin's astonishingly level central plain stands open only to the Gulf of Tonkin. Hanoi is backed up by the hills comprising the Middle Region, and then interior Tonkin is embraced by mountains which the broad wedge of the Red River Valley cleaves into northeast and southwest ranges roughly equal in area, but quite different in character. Both are extensions of the Yunnan Highlands in extreme southwest China, also the origin of the Red River.

Hanoi is located almost centrally in this section of the country, which roughly corresponds to the territory known for twenty years (1954-1975) as the Democratic Republic of Vietnam, the DRV and North Vietnam. The second largest city in this section is the major port of Haiphong. These two cities are Vietnam's largest industrial centers.

The northern Tonkinese coast, though highly indented, affords few convenient harbors and bays for shipping. Ha Long Bay is dotted with numberless limestone protrusions that abruptly break the surface of the water and rise high above it. Legend made this awesome caprice of nature the home to which the sea serpent returned from predations of Vietnam's enemies.

The range to the south of the Red River, the Annamite Cordillera, runs southeastward from Vietnam's highest point, the peak Fan Si Pan (10,308 ft). It marks the border with Laos and at the same time encroaches on the sea, paralleling the coast through the land of Annam. Southward it descends through a succession of high plateaus known collectively as the Central Highlands. Coffee, tea and rubber thrive here on the rich red soil produced long ago by volcanic activity. These high plateaus, so difficult to approach from the east, slope gently westward until they reach the low plains of the Mekong River Delta just north of Ho Chi Minh City (Saigon), giving distinctive shape to the entire central portion of the country.

ANNAM

The seacoast must be important to a country whose interior is so shallow and often so forbidding. Much of that seacoast lies in Annam, whose farming areas are most extensive in the north, which has only one good harbor — Danang, while the southern coast has a number of sheltering bays, notably Cam Ranh Bay, in a stretch of coast where the land is fragmented, but farmed nevertheless.

Not, it seems, as fertile as the immense southern and northern deltas, whose long rivers carry and dump large burdens of silt filched from soils upstream and perhaps far away, Annam's lowland areas are watered by its own rivers tumbling down from mountains within sight. Just as in the larger deltas, rice cultivation is carried on intensively with irrigation.

This is the route traveled by Vietnam's southward expansion in the seventeenth and eighteenth centuries, which emanated from the northern delta and ended at the country's present border with Cambodia and the Gulf of Siam. The mountains crowd the sea so close, they break the coast into pockets. When intercourse was sporadic and travel was slow, these enclaves carried on a life separate even from each other. This is the territory once occupied by the state of Champa, an artistic culture that left behind impressive Buddhist tombs.

Hué, capital of Annam under the French, is on the Perfumed River, so named from the sweet-smelling tree blossoms, meadow flowers and fragrant roots it collected from upstream vegetation.

The deltas of Annam are chained together by stretches of white sand so pure it is used in glassmaking. Groves of coconut palms fringe these beaches, their dunes held in place by coastal pines. Craggy sites overlooking the sea in Quang Nam Danang, Nghia Binh and Phu Khanh provinces are favorite spots for sand martins, which produce the salival 'swallow' nest so prized in Oriental cuisine; at one time a kilogram of these nests (30 or 40) was worth six tons of rice.

There are three brief times of the year when these habitats attract another special breed — the nest collectors, who approach the caves and grottoes from above, from below, however they can, reaching their hands in blind even though poisonous snakes, attracted by the eggs, are also apt to be on the prowl. Assessing the color and quality of the nests is a science in itself.

The Annamite Cordillera was visible over much of its 625 miles to approaching sailors from Portugal, Holland, France, Spain, India, Britain and other European visitors from seaward. It looms over the narrow littoral with its steep eastern slopes. Behind are the dense upland jungle and forest, sparsely inhabited by tribes whose culture recalls a very distant past. The Vietnamese became accustomed to refer to them as *Moi*, or savages, in the long centuries when the uplands were simply ignored because the terrain and the culture of the people were both unsuited to growing wet rice.

There is not much evidence of savage and inimical attitudes on the part of the mountain people, who seem generally to belong to the live-and-let-live school. But their customs and attitudes are different, and practices such as filing and breaking their teeth into points and enameling them black could have given them a reputation for ferocity in some parts of the lowlands.

But 'savage' was a fair description of the fever-ridden environment these people inhabited. Their slash-and-burn method of agriculture condemned them to a mean, if stable, poverty. Jungle beasts, including tigers, were such a threat they had to protect their horses in stalls that were like tight-fitting crates. Their spiritual world, as real to them perhaps as the physical world, peopled with all manner of animistic personifications, was so full of evils and dangers that it is a wonder they did not live in a perpetual state of anxiety. The French, not indifferent to acquiring certain lands these people occupied, used a more neutral and accurate appelation, referring to them simply as Montagnards, or 'hill people'. U.S. soldiers in Vietnam, trying their best to fit the unfamiliar into a known context, simply called them 'Indians'.

COCHINCHINA

Beyond the reach of the high mountains, the southern section of the country has upland areas rising on the Cambodian or western flank of the Annamite Cordillera, but this region, like Tonkin, also has a large intricately channeled delta at its heart. The effort to manage the Mekong's water to advantage dates back at least to the ancient kingdom of Fu Nan, which occupied these lands from the first to the sixth centuries of our era. When the fields are flooded, there are crazy-quilt expanses where the paddies, rimmed by their earth banks, reflect the sunshine like the uneven panes in a leaded window. The region's lattice of streams and canals link small remote villages with each other and with the metropolitan area of Ho Chi Minh City.

The emperor Gia Long, who reunited the country in 1802, initiated a program in the western provinces to develop the almost uninhabited country taken from Cambodia. When the French took control fifty years later, they pushed this program, and rice production quadrupled between 1870 and 1930. The area became attractive to pioneers from other parts, who poled and sculled sampans on the waterways to reach the new lands with their families fields, which have to be fertilized artificially. Aside from what it leaves on the peasant's field, the Mekong also carries enough silt to add some 200 to 260 feet to the delta every year. One official Vietnamese estimate of the Mekong's annual deposit is one billion cubic meters, or nearly 13 times the amount deposited by the Red River. About one-fourth of this delta is under rice cultivation, making the area one of the world's major rice-growing areas.

CLIMATE

Vietnam is entirely in the tropical latitudes, but just barely. Translated to the western hemisphere, the latitude of its northern border would be on a line with Tampico (Mexico), almost touching the Tropic of Cancer. Its southern end, the tip of the Ca Mau Peninsula, with its steamy swamps and mangrove stands, would be even with Panama City.

The winter monsoon begins in the third or fourth week of October and lasts until spring. In this dry season as much as a month may pass without rain. The rainy season is from mid-May to September.

In the south temperatures hold steady and very hot throughout the year, and a very dry half-year alternates with one that is very wet. In other parts there are variations dependent on altitude above sea level and distance from the coast. Northern Vietnam as far down as Hué differs from parts of lowland Vietnam further south in having a clearly marked winter season. Even so, there are no frosts in January, its coldest month, when the temperature averages near 60° F (15° C) and dips into the 40-50° range. Summer temperatures, however, are in line with those further south.

Typhoons from east of the Philippines threaten the Vietnamese coast during the same June-November season as hurricanes along the East Coast of the United States, with a similar peak in August and September as the southwest monsoon is ending. One difference is that the Atlantic hurricane tracks along the coast, while the typhoon cuts the Vietnamese coast at right angles.

The northern delta supports a second rice crop during what the monsoon pattern dictates as the dry season thanks to the crachin (derived from the French *cracher* — 'to spit'), which the Larousse defines as '*une petite pluie pénétrante*' (a fine penetrating rain) and which the Vietnamese refer to as 'flying rain'. This phenomenon is caused by an eastward shift in the dry northeast trade winds. A dense damp fog covers the countryside in a prolonged drizzle, which usually occurs in episodes of three to five days, but has been known to persist for three continuous weeks in the period from late January to mid-April. Most marked in Tonkin, it occurs with decreasing intensity all the way to Cam Ranh Bay in southern Annam. The crachin is of crucial importance to Tonkin. Not that it produces much precipitation, but by preventing evaporation it does provide sufficient moisture for the peasants to grow a second

10.   In Ho Chi Minh City, a 5-kilo sack of rice (11 lbs) costs two dollars, as against only one dollar in the village markets. The salary of a government official corresponds to roughly 5 U.S. dollars a month, but corruption and black-marketeering are widespread and on the increase.

11.   The docile water buffalo is the sole helper of the Vietnamese peasant in plowing rice fields. During the war, the peasants worked areas close to the battlefield and likely bombing targets of enemy planes under cover of darkness. The crop was known as 'night rice', in contrast to the 'day rice' grown in areas that were safe and out of the way. ▷

annual crop of rice.

The 'Laos winds' are a peculiarity in the weather pattern along the central coast. During the rainy season of the southwest monsoon, warm winds blowing down to the sea off the eastern slopes of the mountains cause a high proportion of clear sky conditions between Nha Trang in the south and Dong Hoi, north of Hué, so that this stretch receives somewhat less precipitation than the upper or lower coasts. If they blow several days running, these winds can be so dry as to scorch crops and suck the moisture from the soil.

NATURAL RESOURCES

Various parts of the mountains that rim Tonkin contain deposits of Vietnam's substantial, if little developed, mineral wealth. The list of commercially workable mineral deposits in the northern and central sections is long (coal, phosphate, ores of tin, copper, lead, zinc, manganese, titanium, chromium, tungsten, and aluminum, graphite, mica, silica sand, limestone, talc and asbestos), but the shortage of investment capital is so desperate that few are being worked. Vietnam's coal reserves are estimated at 20 billion tons. The world's largest open-cut anthracite mine is located at Hong Gay on the Gulf of Tonkin. There are also large offshore oil finds in Tonkin Gulf and off the Ca Mau Peninsula.

Vietnam is still a decidedly agricultural country and seems likely to remain so for some time yet. An expansion of cropland by another 50 percent has been projected, which would put one third of the country's area under cultivation.

Vietnam's forests and timber resources have suffered greatly over the last century. In addition to forest fires and the manifold environmental damage caused by slash-and-burn farming, commercial timber exploitation was unsparing in the French colonial period, especially close to the railroad lines. Good land was cleared by large owners to bring it under cultivation, and displaced small farmers cleared less promising land to resume rice production. Finally, during its involvement in the Indochina Wars, the United States pursued an anti-guerrilla strategy of defoliating forests by spraying herbicides from the air. This affected 20 percent of the area of South Vietnam in the late Sixties, and is a reckonable factor in the decline of timber resources. Nevertheless, half of the northern section section of the country is covered by dense tropical and subtropical forests containing such valuable species as ironwood, eucalyptus, teak, mahogany, ebony, camphor laurel, kapok and jacaranda.

With its extensive coastline, Vietnam claims a very large economic area of the ocean, but half of Vietnam's fish catch in the Eighties, about 1.5 million tons, was classified as low-quality.

Central as Vietnam's rivers are to its agriculture, modern times are also calling upon them for electric power.

12. *The rice paddy is the peasant's universe. All agricultural operations, including irrigation and drainage, are still done by hand. In many fields, small grey stone mounds mark the burial places of peasants killed in the war.*

13

13.   On the high plateau of Buon Ma
Thuot, peasants carry their produce to
the market. The Province of Doc Lac has
a rich variety of agricultural products.
The mountain climate is favorable for
growing coffee, along with rubber and
tea, an important export commodity.

14. A government commune where laborers work for the state. Most of them are persons found guilty of minor offenses who now have to work the land without pay until they have served out their sentence.

15. Intensive cultivation of vegetables on the outskirts of Haiphong. In comparison with the South, the North possesses much more advanced technology. During the war, peasants in the North had to learn to make optimal use of every foot of fertile soil. The help which the North Vietnamese received from their allies over a period of 15 years did not include fresh food. ▷

14

16

16. *Loading stocks of rice into baskets which this peasant woman will carry on a pole across her shoulders, still the only way of transporting grain from one place to another.*

17. Peasant women carrying their loads along the state highway from Da Nang to Hué. Often they are obliged to trudge endless miles in the heat or pouring rain because of lack of transportation.

18. Panoramic view of the area around Da Nang, furrowed by rivers flowing toward the sea from the highlands (high plateaus) in the west. ▷

17

19

19. *A passerby lingers in conversation with a woman working in a rice field. Though rice harvesting is an exhausting task, a constant murmur of voices rises from the fields, especially when women predominate among the workers.*

20.   Peasants cleaning rice on a country road. In this phase of the work, men operate the machines, while the women spread the rice to dry.

21.   The principal highway in Vietnam, which runs along the coast from Hanoi to Ho Chi Minh City, was constructed during French rule. In rural regions, peasants use it either as a threshing floor for rice, or for selling their wares, thus compounding the already difficult traffic conditions. ▷

22

22.23. The longest road in the country which runs from the extreme South to the Chinese border is called simply, number 1. Originally built for two way traffic, for most of its length it is one way as the peasants make use of its asphalt shoulders to dry rice, bamboo and other agricultural products. It is also used for small markets and restaurants. I believe that this highway is the longest market-farm in the world.

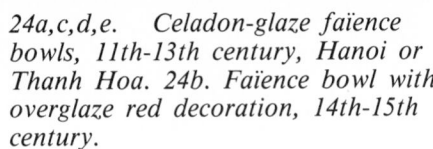

24a,c,d,e. Celadon-glaze faïence bowls, 11th-13th century, Hanoi or Thanh Hoa. 24b. Faïence bowl with overglaze red decoration, 14th-15th century.

25. Vietnamese folk print, a typical example of this popular art form providing pictures, often on Buddhist themes, for the decoration of homes, where they are usually glued to doors and walls.

26a. Faïence bottle with underglaze blue decoration of phoenix and flowers, and intentional crazing (craquelure), 14th-15th century.

26b. Faïence bottle with light yellow overglaze floral decoration, 17th-18th century.

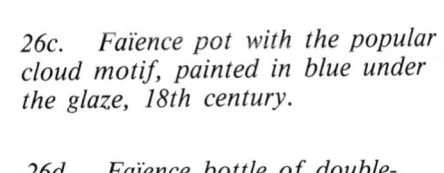

26c. Faïence pot with the popular cloud motif, painted in blue under the glaze, 18th century.

26d. Faïence bottle of double-gourd shape with blue underglaze decoration, 18th century.

26e. Earthenware oil jar with partial brown glazing, date uncertain.

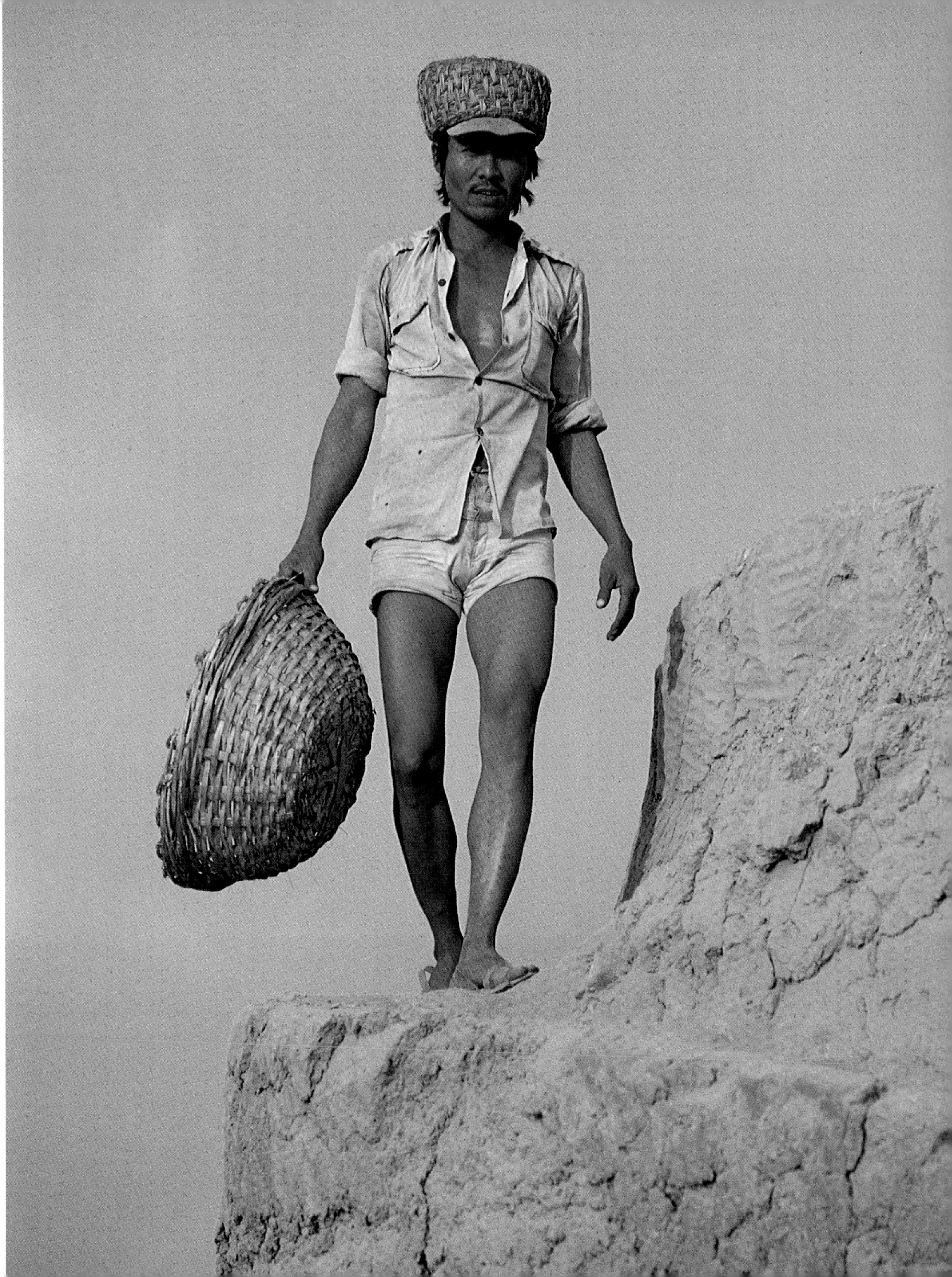

29

27. *Young Montagnards on the porch of their hut. The ethnic minorities in the highlands are estimated to number 8 million people. The outside world became aware of their existence during the war, when the Americans recruited them, taking advantage of their ancient enmity toward the Viets.* ◁

28. *In a primitive cement factory in a suburb of Haiphong, workers carry the material to the top of the furnace in baskets balanced on their heads. In order to survive, this man is obliged to spend all day toiling up and down with the heavy loads.* ◁ ◁

29.	*Path among coconut trees and paddy fields connecting villages of the Tam Ky plain, south of Da Nang.*

30   A scene from the center of
Hué. The old capital city is still
considered by the South Vietnamese
to be the last great city before the
North begins.

30

31. *A brick factory on the outskirts of Haiphong. In a setting reminiscent of a circle in Dante's Inferno, workers carry on their heads the raw materials need to manufacture bricks, a process that was used in Europe over a century ago.*

32. *A small peasant boy traveling alone down the road on his buffalo. I met him 580 miles from Ho Chi Minh City and 8 miles from Da Nang.* ▷

31

33

33. *Peasant returning his flock to their pen at dusk. Poultry is of vital importance to the national diet. Apart from fish, which is rare inland, it is almost the only source of protein. Cattle are extremely scarce. In 1986, UNICEF estimated that the average Vietnamese consumed 1800-1900 calories daily.*

The River of History

EARLIEST TIMES

The history of Vietnam is in many ways similar to its two great rivers. The course of this river of history has it own dangerous and turbulent rapids — those violent periods when the casualties were numerous, nameless and uncounted. It has its stretches of calm water when for a time the land was blessed with good rulers, good neighbors and good weather. Outside influences have joined this river like right and left tributaries, some crucial, others incidental. Finally, this river has its aimless wanderings and bifurcations — times when national purpose and unity were lost or checked, and, like the other two rivers, it has poorly charted upper reaches the explorers have differed over.

Over the last thirty years, while the Vietnamese have been fighting a war of independence and wrestling with intractable problems of defining their identity in modern terms, Vietnamese historians, linguists, physical anthropologists and archeologists have been affirming the nation in their own way.

Ancestors of the present-day Vietnamese were living in the Red River valley when China's Han dynasty extended its dominion over that area in 111 B.C. Everyone agrees on that. But who were they, and were did they come from?

In one picture, formed mainly from Chinese written records, they were a primitive tribal people, much like the uplanders who have survived into the twentieth century. The most extreme version has them settling in this area only two centuries earlier, following their exile from southern China, where they were known as the Yüeh ('Viet' is the Vietnamese pronunciation of the Chinese 'Yüeh', and no one questions this origin of the name). Vietnamese legends tell it differently. They trace the ancestry of the Vietnamese down through a line of Hung kings who ruled this region as the kingdom of Van-lang for long centuries before the third century B.C.

The current scientific view confirms this latter picture. It sees the Vietnamese as the heirs of the Late Bronze-Age culture whose famous decorated bronze drums were unearthed in 1924 at Dong Son, a village on the Ma River in southern Tonkin. Before the Chinese appeared and occupied their area, this people looked southward and eastward toward the sea. That is, they belonged to Southeast Asia in both in their location and their culture. Their

34. *Dusk on the Mekong in 1968. Even then, in times of fierce fighting, the magic colors of sunset suggested a silent truce between the two parties.*

kings ruled in feudal fashion through local men of authority known as the Lac lords. This society had the wealth to support this aristocracy because it grew its rice by irrigation. It was already directing the fresh water pushed back by the ocean tides through an elaborate system of dikes and canals. One of the functions of the Lac lords was to supervise and coordinate the building of these engineering works. Both iron implements and buffaloes were probably used in working the soil.

The next date beyond question is A.D. 39, when the sisters Trung, Lac aristocrats related to the Hung kings, raised a rebellion not put down by the Chinese until A.D. 44. The tale of these women has been a focus of patriotic pride and emulation ever since, every age embroidering it with its own embellishments and attitudes. There is a well-known story from the twelfth century about how the sisters answered prayers for rain. Even the Viet Minh and Viet Cong overlooked the sisters' aristocratic origin and pointed to their example.

THE CHINESE PROVINCIAL PERIOD

In A.D. 42 the veteran general Ma Yuan arrived with a large army and by the year 44 had subdued the rebels and killed thousands of the fighters. In each district captured he set up a proper Chinese administration seeded with Chinese administrators.

General Ma Yuan was a superior civil governor and accomplished a smooth transition to the Chinese system of government. He solidified the conquest by settling his troops in the area as soldier-farmers, a technique the Vietnamese themselves would later use as they extended their own domains southward.

It says something about the resources of the Vietnamese character that this foreign general who defeated and killed the Trung sisters was revered for his subsequent deeds. Centuries later a Chinese governor would claim kinship with him to enhance his prestige with the Vietnamese population. Meanwhile the Chinese approach to public business, grounded in the Confucianist social order of top-down authority, was effectively grafted onto the native culture. Over the next century and a half new settlers and upper-class refugees from political disorders in China established strong families, as did some Vietnamese, perhaps the heirs of the Lac lords, forming the Han-Viet upper class through intermarriage.

Revolts were frequent in this southern province of China. Another rebellion, in A.D. 249, was led by a woman. The Chinese records omit the Lady Trieu, but her memory has survived in the oral history of the Vietnamese as a warrior going into battle on an elephant with her breasts slung over her shoulders. In time the Chinese helpfully redrew provincial borders to coincide with the area inhabited by the Vietnamese. In the early sixth century Ly Bon, a Chinese military governor, declared himself 'Emperor of Nam Viet'. Although he named his realm 'Ten Thousand Springtimes' and his residence 'Ten Thousand Life Spans', these pretensions were snuffed out as soon as the Chinese Empire had negotiated the disorderly transition from the Sui to the great T'ang dynasty.

The final centuries of Vietnam's Chinese provincial experience roughly coincide with the reign of the T'ang dynasty in China (618-907). China's culture enjoyed a golden age in this period of renewed unity. The T'ang also left an indelible mark on Vietnamese life, yet that impact was often harshly imposed and enforced under military governors who became increasingly corrupt and tyrannical, fomenting with one hand the constant rebellion which they suppressed with the other. The end of the T'ang splintered China once again in the early tenth century.

Ngo Quyen was at that time yet another Vietnamese leader targeted by yet another military expedition into Vietnamese lands. The Chinese planned to penetrate the interior up the Bach-dang River before disembarking their seaborne troops. Ngo Quyen thwarted the plan by planting an underwater obstacle in the river. His shallow-draft boats went out at high tide to taunt the Chinese fleet and then retreat, luring the enemy into the estuary. As the tide fell, the heavy Chinese vessels became lodged on the barrier, pinned in a helpless position which Ngo Quyen exploited with flaming arrows. This victory made a tale that was not lost on a people with a keen oral tradition, and when he declared himself king the following spring the Vietnamese began to look to broader national horizons.

INDEPENDENCE

Although that battle initiated an independence lasting nine centuries, the early years were shaky. A promising leader, Dinh Bo Linh, established his capital at a site, Hoa Loa, that could be defended against the inevitable Chinese attempt to reimpose provincial status. He pursued that same end with his Ten Circuit Army, a peasant militia in ten districts of the Red River plain that would mobilize a total of 100,000 peasants. These precautions proved reliable in 981 when Bo Linh's assassination occasioned a new Chinese penetration.

In 1010 Ly Cong Uan established the first of the two lengthy dynasties that were to rule Vietnam as the land of Dai Viet until 1400. Only the scope and flavor of the many notable Ly precedents and permanent institutions can be suggested. The flavor, incidentally, was quite often Chinese. The Vietnamese learned to stomach Chinese ways from the hand of their own rulers. The taxes levied by the Ly on village common lands, on domestic and foreign trade, and on a sensitive commodity like salt, were the first the Vietnamese peasant was ever called upon to pay to his own rulers. Those revenues were used in part to build centralized stockpiles of rice — for the army naturally, but also for famine relief. And roads were built, so that couriers could maintain a rudimentary mail service.

Other public works included flood control embankments along the Red River, and the government promoted agriculture by encouraging expansion of the area under cultivation and by furloughing soldiers to till the land.

The Ly were interested in innovations, and their ambassadors found ways to bring back even the knowhow which the Chinese refused to release. But the most far-reaching Chinese import was not a product of early industrial espionage. The creation of the civil service, indispensable to a centralized administration, capped a series of moves that began in 1070 with the founding of the Temple of Literature, an institution dedicated to the study of Confucianism. Later in the decade a national school was opened in the grounds of the Temple, and the first examinations were held for entry into public service. Both concentrated on the Confucian classics. No institution better exemplifies the classic Chinese and Confucianist style of government than these examinations, which were used to fill vacancies throughout the public administration — from the prime minister right on down to the village clerk. Hanoi was chosen as capital for its central location, and Vietnam had a true central government.

Meanwhile, the expansion southward — which would cease only when it reached the Gulf of Siam (Thailand) in the eighteenth century — had commenced at the expense of the Buddhist state of Champa, which in 1069 was forced to cede three of its northern provinces.

By the end of the twelfth century, the Ly had spent its vitality. Taxes had become burdensome and were going for royal debauches. The Tran dynasty, which took over in a transition spiked with perfidy and violence, initiated an equally lengthy reign (1225-1400).

Kublai Khan, the Mongol emperor of China, tested the Tran early with three invasions in their first sixty years. On the third occasion, Tran Hung Dao defeated a Mongol-Chinese army perhaps half a million strong and an immense fleet. The odd thing is that he did it by repeating his predecessor's trick of maneuvering the Mongol fleet onto iron-tipped stakes in the same river. Can the Chinese have been so forgetful?

The fourteenth was a century of wars with Champa, which by 1312 had been reduced in size and status. But a decade later it rebounded under a vigorous new king, who invaded Vietnam repeatedly and in 1371 even pillaged the capital. The dynasty that had thrown back the Mongols was clearly in decline. By mid-century feudal lords were challenging the emperor and warring with smaller landowners. Peasant uprisings became more frequent. At court the Buddhists, spiritual tutors and advisers of kings until the thirteenth century, were at odds with the scholar-bureaucrats produced by the Confucianist system of examinations.

In 1400 General Ho Qui Ly seized power and strove to restore central authority and resolve the country's internal crisis with reforms. He limited the amount of land a family could own and rented excess state land to landless peasants. He printed proclamations in Vietnamese instead of Chinese and opened free schools in provincial capitals. Soon the deposed Tran family, the threatened feudal lords, and emissaries from Champa raised a chorus for Chinese intervention. The Ming dynasty answered these entreaties by invading in 1407.

For twenty years the Chinese again ruled Vietnam as a province. This time they were even more bent on erasing Vietnamese culture and jamming this intractable group into the Chinese ethnic mosaic. They seized the literary and historical manuscripts in the national archives and hauled them off to China. They humiliated the local population by forcing men to wear their hair long and women to dress in the Chinese style. Betel chewing, a custom universal in Southeast Asia, was forbidden.

Centuries of independence and the hammering of Chinese invasions had forged in the Vietnamese a clearly defined identity and strong resolve neither to become nor to be treated as Chinese. In 1418 the patriot Le Loi again prefigured twentieth-century events by going into the mountains with a small band to build a resistance movement. He was joined there by a well-known poet, Nguyen Trai, who became his lieutenant in a campaign that achieved final success in 1428.

Le Loi could not recover the priceless national legacy which the Chinese had stolen and destroyed, but he was able to build institutions to consolidate the nationalist sentiment that had driven the powerful northern neighbor back over the mountains. An agriculture devastated and disrupted by decades of rebellion and warfare had to be restored, then expanded as towns and population grew. All available land was brought under cultivation, and further conquest opened up new land in the south. By 1471 Champa was holding on to its two last districts.

Le Loi pointed a direction in land reform, taxation, and limitation of large estates that would be followed by his remarkable successor later in the century, Le Thanh Ton (1460-1497), whose reign name was Hong Duc ('Great Virtue'). The legal code he adopted was the most progressive in Southeast Asia at the time, though largely a rewrite of China's Confucianist system. The Le rulers founded their dynasty on expulsion of the Chinese, but they worked to reinforce authority with Confucianist institutions. However, the new code did include distinctively Vietnamese features, notably greater rights and status for women — in society, under the law, and in the family.

After Le Thanh Ton's death the Le dynasty went through ten monarchs in thirty years. A powerful family named Mac seized the weakly held throne. Two other families, the Nguyen and Trinh, rose up as challengers. In 1545 their combined forces defeated the Mac and cut off the southern part of the country. By the end of the century they had supplanted the Mac in the north, and the Trinh took the ascendancy. The Nguyen agreed to govern the southern provinces, but in 1620 achieved autonomy in the south by refusing to send tax collections northward.

Thus, two families claiming loyalty to the same powerless sovereign ruled the two halves of the country: the Trinh with its capital at Hanoi and the Nguyen at Hué. For fifty years they warred with one another. European merchants reaching these parts were quick to make themselves useful by supplying arms, the Portugese in the south and the Dutch in the north. Both watched their profits dry up when the two sides declared a stalemate in 1672.

The century of peace between these two ruling families did not signify general tranquility. Hunger for land became desperate as large holdings were amassed, leaving more and more peasants landless. This problem was worse in the north, since there were no new rice lands to spread to, and peasant uprisings kept the rulers pinned to the battlefield from 1739 to 1770. The Nguyen in the south simply took land away from the Cham and Khmer kingdoms. But they were not spared peasant rebellion either. By the mid-Sixties armed peasant detachments were operating against the feudal lords.

The Tay Son detachment, so called from the mountains it came from in central Vietnam, was led by three brothers who were not peasants, but educated members of the minor aristocracy. The battlecry of the rebellion they led was 'Take from the rich, share among the poor!' In 1783 they defeated the Nguyen in a decisive battle and then turned their rebellion northward against the Trinh. Except for small areas on the southern coast to which the Nguyen had fled, the Tay Son brothers succeeded in uniting the country for the first time in over two centuries. As a token of that unity they perpetuated the Le dynasty in name, but divided the real power among themselves by regions. When the hapless Le heir called in the Chinese, the Tay Son defeated the Manchu invaders and discarded the monarch.

The most active of the brothers, Nguyen Hué, proclaimed himself Emperor Quang Trung in 1789 and set about rebuilding the country's agriculture and improving the lot of the peasantry. His death in 1792 cut short another ambitious reign and left another power vacuum, which would be filled by Vietnam's last dynasty, the Nguyen (1802-1945). In their second campaign against the Nguyen, the Tay Son forces had killed their ruler and his immediate family. The sole survivor was a nephew, Nguyen Anh, a boy of sixteen, who fled into the Mekong Delta with the help and under the tutelage of a Frenchman, Pigneau de Béhaine, Bishop of Adran. There he took over leadership of a band of Nguyen loyalists and beginning in 1784 waged what is called the Monsoon War against the Tay Son. In the summer he would send his boats up the coast with the southwest trade filling their sails. The winter monsoon would bring them south again. By 1801, Nguyen Anh had regained Hué, and he captured Hanoi a year later.

Nguyen Anh clung to defense and Confucianism in dealing with the uncertainties of the nineteenth century. Even in his rebel base camp he had set up a proper Confucianist government and held proper Confucianist examinations to staff his administration. He renounced Hanoi as his capital, although it had been the seat of every emperor since the eleventh century. Instead he nodded north and south in the cosmetic detail of his name as ruler, Gia Long (Gia Dinh, near Saigon, and Thang Long for Hanoi). Hué was a central location for an emperor who intended to repair a lengthy breach. Moreover, his family had ruled there for generations, and it had good natural protection — mountains on three sides and a river to the sea too shallow for seagoing craft.

Gia Long was a vigorous ruler. He rebuilt a country that had suffered thirty years of war, and brought new land under cultivation. But he did not respond to the problems that had led to the Tay Son Rebellion. In seeking national unity he looked instead to a strong central state immune to the kind of split he had just repaired. The privileged classes were still exempted from taxation, from military service and from the labor conscription Gia Long used to carry out his public works program and the lead item on his personal agenda — the imperial city at Hué. These burdens were borne exclusively by the peasantry, who lost under the Nguyen even the modest gains made under the Tay Son.

A new legal code undid the adaptations to Vietnamese society and custom contained in the 350-year-old Hong Duc Code. Edicts were issued requiring Chinese style of dress, a measure fifteenth-century Vietnamese had considered tyrannical. And prohibitions were placed on Buddhism, Taoism and native religions, not to mention Christianity, which by 1841 may have had as many a half a million adherents.

In the 1830s the Catholics in the south supported a revolt against the central government. Gia Long's successor, Minh Mang, crushed the rebellion and then ordered reprisals against the south. After that he saw the Catholics as a threat to the state. In time, as the Western presence in Asia increased, the Nguyen hardened and broadened this anti-Christian attitude into a general anti-Western stance.

Toward mid-century the French, armed with mistreatment of missionaries and Christians as an excuse, seriously undertook repeated military action in quest of special trade privileges. The naval firepower is sent upriver to the cities finally made that demand stick with Emperor Tu Duc, but the weakness of his position was predetermined by the conservative and defensive posture taken from the beginning of the century.

FRENCH COLONIALISM

By 1897 forty years of warfare and strongarm diplomacy had given France full possession of Cochinchina (Cochin China) as an outright colony, while Annam and Tonkin became protectorates. All resistance supporting the Vietnamese emperor had been beaten in the field. French interests were finally ready to administer and transform Indochina. They expected high returns for French investors and cheap raw materials for French industry — rubber, hard coal, iron, tin and timber. The rub was that economic

35. A junk glides upon the waters
of Ha Long Bay in the setting sun.
These vessels with colorful stiff
sails, once typical of the China Sea,
now survive only in Vietnam.
Fishermen use them to sail among
the isles of the bay, which are full
of caves where pirates used to hide
in past centuries.

development required public money for roads and railroads to carry those materials and seaports equipped for transocean vessels. Yet anti-colonial sentiment in France was too strong for them to lobby for large appropriations.

The French governors-general strove until World War I to finance those projects by taxing the native population, which meant the peasantry. Not only did the peasants have to work as conscript labor, there was a head tax and taxes on land, salt and alcohol to pay. The taxes hurt even more because they were collected in money, not rice, the traditional form of payment. Virtually a stranger to cash, not to mention savings, the peasant traditionally borrowed just to plant his crop. French policies drove the peasants to borrow even more, and moneylenders exploited their helplessness with usurious rates and ultimately took their land.

To develop large-scale commercial farming in the north, the French would have needed to solve the overpopulation which has given the Communist regime such nightmares. They looked instead to the south, where they raised cash crops of tea, coffee and rubber on the fertile slopes and rice in the lowlands.

The mid-1920s brought a fresh infusion of capital into Indochina as a new French plan was launched to exploit the colony. Rubber plantations were being developed on huge tracts ceded to the country's corporations in a stretch extending from the South China Sea to the Mekong River in Cambodia. One was Phu Rieng, a Michelin tract eight miles wide and ten miles long. The chilling cries of the gibbons resounded as unskilled laborers cleared the tropical rain forest, wielding hand tools against giant teaks and tungs, uncertain which way to run when the trees came crashing down.

The story of Tran Tu Binh, an eighteen-year-old peasant from Tonkin who became a leader of the famous Phu Rieng strike in 1930, provides the counterpoint and underside of the development strategy pursued by the French. His memoir, covering the years 1926-1930, suggests some of the reasons for the rise of revolutionary Communism in Vietnam: French attitudes and practices, the poverty of the peasants, and the nationalism and unsatisfied thirst for education of young Vietnamese who had received some schooling.

In 1930, which opened a decade that prefigured Vietnam's revolutionary future, Tu Binh's personal account of events at Phu Rieng ties into national events like a small tributary joining the mainstream of Vietnamese history. The strike of 5000 workers at Phu Rieng in February 1930 sparked uprisings in towns and cities throughout the country. The French clapped thousands of nationalists and social rebels in jail and deported them to the penal colony on Poulo Condore. Tran Tu Binh was among them. Many naive young rebels like him would get the focus and education for the revolutionary struggle from older party regulars in prison. Before the year was out Ho Chi Minh would bring the three separate Communist organizations together to form the Indochinese Communist Party.

36. Limestone peaks rising from the sea make an impressive landscape on Ha Long Bay. The largest rock, some 1000 feet high, is called Poetry Rock, because for centuries Vietnamese scholars sought seclusion on it when they wanted to write or meditate. ▷

37

37. *Inland from Ha Long Bay extends an area rich in minerals where some of Vietnam's few industries have developed. Cargo vessels are forced to load and unload in the middle of the bay with the help of these large transport junks, since the small port is not adequately equipped.*

38.   Woman sailor. Equality of the sexes
is a declared principle in Vietnam.
Women can often be seen performing
heavy physical labor.

39, 40.   The color of dawn over Ha
Long Bay. It is certain to become one of
the major attractions once tourism
develops in Vietnam. A plan to build
four new hotels already exists, but is held
up for lack of funds. At the moment,
Ho Chi Minh City, formerly Saigon, is
the place most visited by foreigners,
thanks to the good accommodation
available.

39

42

42.   A junk sails expertly between the islets of Ha Long. Handling such a craft is an art in itself, for the wind plays tricks as it passes between the islands.

43

41.   Woman maneuvering her fishing boat. Most inhabitants of Ha Long Bay spend all their lives aboard their junks and are expert boatmen, as are the inhabitants of the Mekong Delta.

43.   Village near Hong Gay on Ha Long Bay. The houses built on rocks resemble Mediterranean architecture. Although only a few miles from China, these communities have preserved their own culture, quite different from that of their mighty neighbor.

44.   Fishing fleet at Nha Trang. A major part of Vietnam's industrial fishing catch has to be exported in exchange for much needed foreign currency. ▷

45. View of the port of Ho Chi Minh City. The best-equipped port in all of Vietnam, it was constructed by the French, rebuilt by the Americans, and remains today the only large port of the South.

46. Vietnamese begin a new day by exercising on a promenade in Ho Chi Minh City. In spite of poor living conditions, physical exercise has retained its traditional importance.

45

46

47. *Standing on the prow, the smiling captain of this passenger boat poses for my camera.*

48. *Crowded ferry crossing the river near Ho Chi Minh City.*

49

50

51

49, 50, 51 *During the war Ha Long was the second most important North Vietnamese port. The lack of proper mooring facilities forced the Vietnamese ships to unload in the middle of the bay using junks and barges. This practice is still in use today. Continual air raids during the war made this both a dangerous and ingenious operation as the Vietnamese were forced to work at night.*

War and More War

JAPANESE OCCUPATION AND THE AUGUST REVOLUTION

In 1940 the Japanese occupied Indochina and used it to launch major operations in Southeast Asia. They left the running of it to the Vichy French administration. In March 1945, with defeat a certainty, they jailed French officialdom in a body, hoping this lightning coup would remove France from the region's future. As a replacement they allowed Bao Dai, last of the Nguyen, to set up a government in Hué.

Those short months from March to August 1945 counted for much in the fortunes of the Viet Minh, the coalition for national independence which the ICP (Indochinese Communist Party) put together in 1941. Ho Chi Minh himself spent 1942-43 in a Chinese prison, but his organization was active during the war years in the mountain area it controlled. In late 1944 he returned to Vietnam, where his anti-Japanese stance brought aid and advisers from the United States in exchange for intelligence on Japanese movements and help in returning downed flyers.

This gave the Viet Minh the tactical advantage of being alone in the field when the war ended. When Hiroshima and Nagasaki were bombed, the ICP called for a general uprising. On September 2 Ho Chi Minh read the declaration of independence of the Democratic Republic of Vietnam in Hanoi on behalf of the Viet Minh. Bao Dai, perpetual figurehead, abdicated.

Indochina had not been forgotten in the wartime deliberations of the Allies. Roosevelt was against reinstalling France in its colonial domains, but the United States did agree to the British accepting the Japanese surrender south of the 16th Parallel and the Chinese north of it. In its sector Britain supported the French claim and even resorted to Japanese military help in overcoming local resistance. Under British cover the French took control in Saigon and dispatched forces to regain control of the countryside.

One year after the Japanese removed the French administration, the French recognized the DRV as a 'free state' in the Indochinese Federation and the French Union. Ho in return did not oppose French forces when they came north of the 16th parallel. His own organization was at odds on this point. France was not offering sovereignty, but paper independence, designed to placate

52. *A section of the Nha Trang canal. In the Sixties, the headquarters of the Green Berets was in this city, and all their military operations originated here. No remains of the old base survive.*

the American conscience in what amounted to its support of colonialism.

During the summer of 1946 Ho and the French did a diplomatic dance, both playing for time. Ho knew that the colonial idea was a casualty of the war so that time was on his side in the long run. The French were assembling their forces.

LA GUERRE D'INDOCHINE

The inevitable spark was struck in November when a French gunboat fired on people thronging the quay in Haiphong. On December 19 the Viet Minh issued its own declaration of war by attacking the French garrison in Hanoi. The First Indochina War, *La Guerre d'Indochine*, would be fought until the spring of 1954.

The Viet Minh had powerful popular support. In Confucianist terms it had demonstrated its 'virtue'. Not only had it stood up to France, but its organizational abilities had so impressed people that they felt Communist leadership would help to even the odds. When France saw it would be facing a serious military opponent, it set up Bao Dai once again and granted independence and unity on paper.

Military aspects took ascendancy over diplomatic issues. Vo Nguyen Giap, General Giap for short, bested the French in the far northern mountains along the Chinese border. The U.S. essayed to improve Bao Dai's political credibility, which was understandably low after a decade spent in puppet harness. Bao Dai went on proclaiming the concessions of independence and unity he had won from France, and the Viet Minh continued to win on the battlefield and to prosper politically. Starting in 1947 the nationalist coalition had begun to lose some of its non-Communist adherents, but as the war progressed, it was gaining support that went far broader and deeper than political alliances. It had inspired in young peasants an invincible readiness for any effort and any sacrifice. By 1953 the French were seeking negotiations, and talks were scheduled in Geneva. The most resounding statement of those talks would be made the day before they opened by a non-participant, General Giap, in an out-of-the-way place called Dien Bien Phu.

In the valley of Dien Bien Phu — dimensions: eleven miles by three — war became the ultimate game of chess. This tiny village in northwestern Vietnam was astride the Viet Minh's supply route from China for its offensive underway in Laos. General Navarre, the newly arrived French commander in Indochina, turned the village into a fortress with the intent of luring the Viet Minh forces onto the flats of this valley.

Two French miscalculations proved to be crucial. First, they believed Giap did not have the logistical support to mass the forces required to take the fortified camp. Coolie transport, they calculated, could never carry the rice to feed four divisions. The French had broken the Viet Minh supply code, but they did not pick up on the 2000 Peugeot bicycles that were requisitioned. Those jury-rigged bicycles made giants of the coolies. Poles bound to the frame with rags allowed the coolie to walk or trot behind a bicycle that burned no fuel and could be loaded with 450 pounds of rice, gun parts or artillery shells. After delivery, the coolie would return the chain to the sprockets and pedal back for another load.

The other French assumption was that the Viet Minh could not exploit the camp's vulnerability to hill guns. When the French colonel in charge of the camp's artillery realized at the start of the bombardment that the Viets had not only lifted heavy guns into place, but had excavated tunnels that made their artillery invulnerable, he pulled the pin from a grenade and held it next to his heart.

'NAM

By the mid-Fifties containment of Communism had become the overriding principle in global United States foreign policy. The Korean War had demonstrated the particular point it put on this strategy in Asia. Before Dien Bien Phu, United States involvement in the Indochinese imbroglio was not direct or very public, but it had been a keenly interested party behind the scenes at every stage. American aid had kept the French going in their war against the Viet Minh. When the fate of Dien Bien Phu was still not altogether sealed, the French had requested direct American intervention. Consideration was given to removing the Viet Minh artillery from positions above Dien Bien Phu with atomic bombs, but President Eisenhower refused the request by putting conditions which France could not accept.

The refusal to intervene on behalf of France did not signify that Washington was turning aside; on the contrary, from that point on the United States moved to displace France in Indochina. Ultimately it would make a deeper commitment than France and would become more treacherously involved.

The first step taken by the U.S. in countering the Viet Minh in the south was to remove the anti-French motive from the equation. During the Geneva negotiations the U.S. prevailed on the pro-French Bao Dai to choose Ngo Dinh Diem for prime minister because he had stood up to the French. Within months of becoming prime minister, Diem had displaced Bao Dai and got himself elected president of the Republic of South Vietnam. In early 1956 he had the French remove their remaining troops, and he set about dismantling the Viet Minh structure in South Vietnam.

The Geneva Accords called for elections throughout Vietnam in January 1956. Certain that the Viet Minh would carry that election, Hanoi felt it could ignore Diem for a time. Diem's methods were effective against his opponents in the south, but they were not improving his popularity. He was in fact making enemies so rapidly that the Viet Cong (the Communist insurgency in South Vietnam) later saw him as a great asset to its cause and was cool toward the prospect of his removal. In time Hanoi realized that Diem's indifference to his own popularity meant that he had no intention of submitting to an election. They could not afford to sit idly by while he and his brother Ngo Dinh Nhu used the secret police to destroy their entire organization in the south.

Diem's unpopularity made him more and more dependent on the United States, which had succeeded France as sponsor of the Saigon regime. In 1962 Diem and his advisers pursued a version of the strategic hamlet program. The idea was to deny the Viet Cong access to the peasants by herding them into guarded camps. The peasants disliked the project from the moment they were recruited to build the camps. Often they were moved considerable distances from their homes, their fields and the graves of their ancestors. Moreover, the plan did nothing toward land reform, an issue on which Diem favored the rich and the big landowners.

But this was only one of the snowballing failures of the Diem regime, which answered the increasing resistance with ever more severe repression. Between the spring and fall of 1963 the regime waged outright war on the Buddhists: raiding pagodas, killing many Buddhist monks and priests, and arresting thousands of others. Demonstrations at Saigon University in August led to large-scale arrests and the closing of Saigon and Hué universities. In June the first Buddhist monk showered himself with gasoline from a plastic can and immolated himself. Six others would do the same in the months that followed. The street scene in which a man in yellow robes is instantly engulfed by flames had a visual power even a world public inured to violence could not stomach.

In the latter months of 1963 the Kennedy Administration apprised South Vietnamese generals that it would welcome a change. A military takeover in November assassinated Diem and his brother. Over the next five years a succession of generals took up the reins of government in Saigon, but none was able to consolidate his power until General Nguyen Van Thieu took over with Air Marshal Ky as his partner in the latter Sixties. By that time the U.S. was fully committed in Vietnam.

In the year and a half that followed Diem's death decisions to escalate the war were made in Hanoi and Washington. Between March 1965, when the first U.S. Marines landed at Danang, and March 1968, when Lyndon Johnson declared he would not seek re-election, the United States answered Hanoi's combined political and military struggle with a combined strategy of its own.

On the military side it rapidly increased troop strength: 350,000 by mid-1966, just under half a million by the middle of 1967, to a peak of over half a million in early 1968. The tonnage of bombs dropped in that three-year period was twice that dropped during World War II; more than two-thirds of the villages in the North were bombed; the devastation in rural areas of the South was so intense that refugees fled in overwhelming numbers to the cities.

During this hottest and most terrible period of the war, the type of warfare was changing. The First Indochina War had been a revolutionary war. The army that beat the French grew directly out of the Viet Minh insurgency. In the Second Indochina War the native insurgent element of the South could hold its own in the countryside, but failed to generate much support in the cities. It could not stage, much less win, large battles against the highly mobile American forces. It was an authentic insurgency with popular support, but President Thieu's 1970 land reform deprived it of a key issue with the peasants. It suffered many setbacks from the counter-insurgency strategy and was increasingly given the role of a mere adjunct to the Hanoi military machine.

Southern leaders in Viet Cong organizations sensed an overbearing and arrogant attitude in the North Vietnamese they worked with. Attuned as they were to the political and economic realities of southern society, they perceived northern attitudes to be increasingly dogmatic, fanatical and anti-southern. This pattern would become obvious and dominant after unification.

During 1966 and part of 1967 North Vietnamese armed forces attempted direct engagement of the ARVN [Army of South Vietnam] and U.S. forces, but losses were too great. Thereafter, they punctuated a tactical defensive stance with strategic offensives: the Tet Offensive in 1968, the 1972 Easter Offensive, and the Final Push that resulted in the fall of Saigon and the collapse of South Vietnam in 1975.

THE TET AND EASTER OFFENSIVES

General Giap's design of the countrywide offensive in January 1968 contained two elements. The northern fire bases at Khe Sanh and Loc Ninh were attacked on January 10. The hope behind this feint was that General Westmoreland would anticipate a North Vietnamese invasion over the 17th parallel and draw forces off from the cities, which were the real target. Meanwhile the Viet Cong pumped men and arms into the cities when the stream of holiday travelers made security lax. In the best case, the planners thought, they would spark a general uprising that could bring down the government of South Vietnam.

Meanwhile, the fighting at Khe Sanh was serious. The base had been left a shambles after the first night's barrage of rocket, mortar and machine-gun fire, and was highlighted on the evening news in the United States. The resemblance to Dien Bien Phu made it all the more necessary to hold out. U.S. troops were taken away from the southern cities and sent north.

On the night between January 30 and 31 the real offensive exploded within 40 major cities and towns in every corner of South Vietnam. U.S. intelligence had been expecting a large offensive for some time, but clearly that expectation did not diminish the element of surprise. The impact on the population of South Vietnam and on the American public was immense. Optimistic accounts meant to persuade people that the war was being won came winging back like vicious boomerangs as people saw film clips of American diplomats covered with blood and guerrillas roaming the grounds of the U.S. Embassy in Saigon.

American forces had built up to over half a million men, requests were pending for some 200,000 more, and yet official spokesmen could not sell the proposition that the war was winnable. The war was not over, American forces would not be fully withdrawn for another four years, but a mortal blow had been dealt to American resolve.

The Tet Offensive did not succeed in detonating a popular uprising in the cities. In some towns the violence set off by infiltrators and outside forces that joined them flared up and was soon extinguished. In others, notably Hué and Ben Tre, the NVA [North Vietnamese Army] and Viet Cong forces offered tough resistance. The U.S. officer who commanded the retaking of Ben Tre remarked memorably, ''We had to destroy the town in order to save it.'' Hué was taken back on February 25, but not before naval and air bombardment had ravaged the Old City.

By early March all towns had been cleared of invaders. Hanoi had paid with heavy losses, but the ultimate political and diplomatic gains were incalculable.

In mid-1971 negotiations started by the Nixon Administration were bogged down. Washington said it would withdraw unilaterally if Hanoi would stop infiltrating the South. Hanoi said it would accept a coalition government in Saigon followed by a ceasefire and United States troop withdrawal. The sticking point was whether President Thieu would head the new government.

Time passed. By early 1972 the United States had only token ground forces left in Vietnam. Hanoi surveyed the battleground. Certain that the United States would not re-enter the ground war, although still providing air support to the South Vietnamese Army, it decided fighting would do more than talking to change the terms of the discussion.

It named the campaign it launched at the onset of the rainy season after Nguyen Hué, ablest of the Tay Son brothers. This invasion in strength drove three prongs into the long body of South Vietnam. On March 30 a tank and infantry force of 40,000 attacked the coast just below the 17th parallel. In five days it took all of Quang Tri Province except the capital. On April 5 the southern prong struck near Tay Ninh and An Loc, only 65 miles northwest of Saigon. A cover of bad weather delayed U.S. response. When it delivered its immense bombardment, its planes faced surface-to-air missiles, and MiGs attacked the 7th Fleet, which stood off the coast. On April 23 the central thrust toward Kontum in the Central Highlands also came during weather bad enough to hold off air support. Four days later the offensive in the north was renewed, and Quang Tri fell on May 1. But the North Vietnamese forces were prevented from continuing their drive to Hué. In the delta the Viet Cong was attacking provincial capitals with rockets, and North Vietnamese forces moved to within 40 miles of Saigon.

On May 8 the United States mined North Vietnamese ports,

including Haiphong, and by end-May the tide was turning. The North Vietnamese were retreating from Kontum. The seige of An Loc was lifted on June 18. By the end of June a counter-offensive was being mounted in the north, but it was not until September 19 that the city of Quang Tri was retaken. By that time it had been more or less flattened by air bombardment.

The campaign had lasted six months. Hanoi had committed everything it had, but had not brought down the Thieu regime. Yet time was on its side. In October both sides had taken different negotiating positions. If Washington was willing to withdraw without requiring withdrawal of North Vietnam's forces, Hanoi would accept Thieu's presidency of a future Saigon government. The agreement ending the war and restoring peace in Vietnam was signed in Paris on January 27, 1973. President Thieu protested that he had been abandoned.

THE FINAL PUSH

U.S. air power had saved the south in the 1972 Easter Offensive, which proved the failure, not the success, of the program to transfer the burden of national defense to the fatally flawed South Vietnamese Army. This corrupt organization was designed more for protecting the regime than waging war.

The last American combat troops were withdrawn in the spring of 1973. During 1974 the North Vietnamese made gains in the South. The battlefield situation was developing to their advantage. The Ho Chi Minh Trail was now a highway whose surface had been hardened with crushed rock, and a fuel pipeline ran along it. Food prices in South Vietnam were rising at a rate higher than 300 percent, and the government's soldiers were moonlighting to make ends meet. As the flow of dollars dried up, unemployment compounded the problem of overcrowding in the cities already made acute by refugees, especially in Saigon. Corruption was rampant, and internal discontent was growing more intense and spreading contagiously from one segment of society to another.

Meanwhile, the general staff in Hanoi was anxious to prepare a combat plan for the coming year. Above all it wanted to capture territory from which to launch the final blow in 1976. The first piece it went after was the northern half of Phuoc Long Province, north of Saigon. By early January it held the entire province. The surprising ease of this capture did not alter the two-year battle plan except to add a proviso that an opportunity presenting itself to take Saigon in 1975 would be followed up. Hoping to cut South Vietnam in half, in March it centered a strike on Ban Me Thuot in the Central Highlands. This small city was not the scene of the last fighting, but the battle fought there was the last real one of the war.

President Thieu, himself a general, reacted to the defeat at Ban Me Thuot by ordering a strategic withdrawal of forces from the highlands and from Quang Tri to protect the coastal cities and the

53. Scrap pile of U.S. aircraft, an exhibit of the Military Museum in Hanoi. A Vietnamese MiG 21 is placed on top of the pile, with obvious symbolism. The Vietnamese claim to have shot down 358 U.S. planes over Hanoi from 1966 to the end of December 1972. The remains of a B52 still lie on the bottom of a pond on the outskirts of Hanoi.

south. This decision had a disastrous effect. Panic seized both civilians and military. North Vietnamese units redirected their line of attack northward to Danang, which was in a state of chaos as Boeing 727s were being used to lift out American advisers and some South Vietnamese forces. The success was so rapid, the question was whether Hanoi could react quickly enough to take full advantage of it in the few weeks left before the rains. On April 21 the last tough resistance collapsed at Xuan Loc, and later in the day President Thieu resigned. In the ten days that followed North Vietnamese forces surrounded the capital, prepared what was called the Ho Chi Minh Campaign to liberate Saigon, and took the panicked and weakly defended city as the Americans rushed their evacuation effort at the Tan Son Nhut airfield.

POSTWAR TROUBLES

By any account Vietnam's experience since the fall of Saigon has been one of the most melancholy in this people's very long history. The economic problems were of such magnitude that no amount of foreign aid or popular enthusiasm could have made it an easy time. The war did more than disrupt farming life, it ripped up the land itself. The cities were in chaos. The stream of refugees first from the North and then from the countryside had swollen city populations out of all proportion. Much of the country's scant industrial facilities had been destroyed or dislocated. The river of American dollars into the South had dried up, and the massive wartime aid from the U.S.S.R. and China was cut back.

At almost the same moment that the government of South Vietnam fell, Communist regimes took over in Laos and Cambodia as well. The three regimes acknowledged a 'special relationship'. But the Khmer Rouge revolutionaries in Cambodia were aberrant Communists bent on summary execution of modern society. Cities were emptied of their inhabitants. Refugee reports of genocide shocked and revolted the entire world.

Vietnam had particular reasons for alarm, for the Pol Pot regime was violently anti-Vietnamese. The sizable Vietnamese minority needed protection. A large tongue of Cambodian territory known as Parrot's Beak plunges into Vietnam. There were border disputes and conflicting claims to islands in the Gulf of Thailand. Twice in 1977 the Khmer Rouge made limited incursions into Vietnamese territory. The Vietnamese responded by crossing the border in force. At this point Pol Pot, adamantly rejecting the *modus vivendi* of a buffer zone, broke off relations, and the clashes continued. Meanwhile, Hanoi hammered together the political framework to replace the Pol Pot regime. In late December 1978 it launched the invasion that would install it in Pnom Penh.

Vietnam paid a high price for securing a friendly regime in Pnom Penh, which the United Nations General Assembly refused to recognize.

54. Remains of a North Vietnamese tank destroyed in heavy fighting in Quang Tri, now used for drying coconut. The massive appearance of these tanks was responsible for the North Vietnamense breakthrough in 1975. After crossing the entire South in the final push, they entered Saigon in triumph. ▷

55. *Even the roof of an old French bunker north of Quang Tri can be used to dry coconut.*

56-58. *The shell of the Catholic church in Quang Tri. Some 20 years after the fierce fighting to recapture the church, it has not been rebuilt. The city fell into North Vietnamese hands on May 1, 1972, and on September 19, with the aid of B52s and U.S. helicopters, the South managed to regain control over it. Quang Tri finally fell in February 1975, during the offensive that brought ultimate victory to Hanoi's forces.*

57

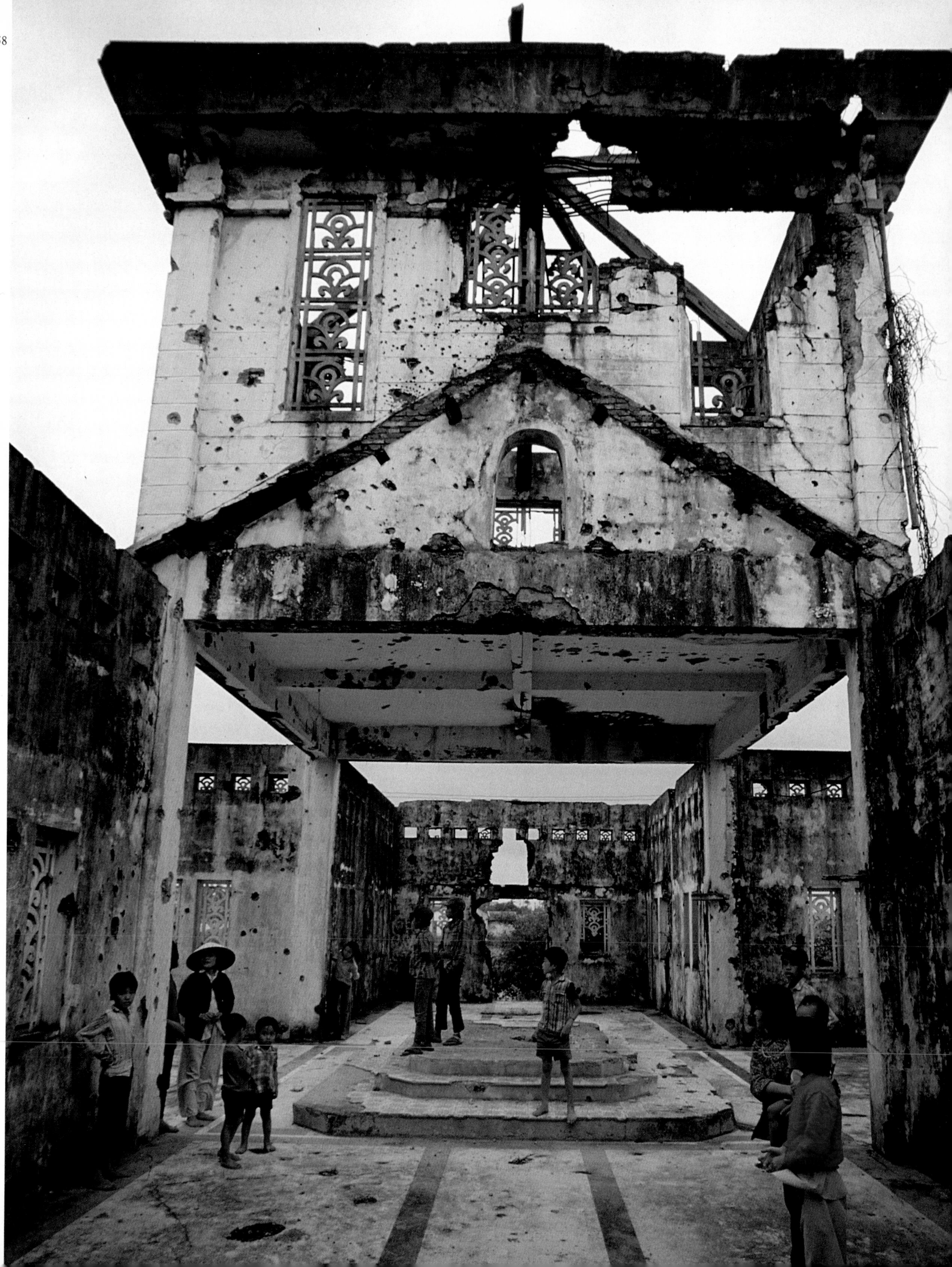

59. Plan of the network of underground tunnels dug by the Viet Cong at Chu Chi; today they are visited by tourists and by Vietnamese youth for educational purposes. The Viet Cong had a very effective network of tunnels, some 18.5 miles in length, going as far as Bien Hoc and the entrance to Saigon. The large U.S. base of the 25th Infantry Division was located above this subterranean maze.

60

60. Bunker at Da Nang. The presence of large quantities of ordnance scattered throughout the country continued to cause accidents years after the war. According to Vietnamese sources, some 200,000 unexploded shells were found in 1975 alone. In the Province of Quang Tri, about 100 people were killed or injured during a two-year period in which 900,000 shells were defused.

61. Inside a tunnel in Chu Chi. This is one of the larger halls which served as hospital quarters. The Viet Cong spent all their time in these insanitary tunnels, which they left only while on attack missions aimed at the nearby military base. The tunnels, mostly 20 inches in diameter, had sections that were mined or led to dead ends.

62. For many Vietnamese children a derelict army vehicle is their only playground. Many of these would have been recycled but for their inaccessible location and lack of transport. Almost all accessible and transportable scrap metal has been purchased by the Japanese for recycling into household electrical appliances.

63. The train that runs between Ho Chi Minh City and Hanoi. It took 4 years to repair all the bridges of Vietnam's principal railroad. Even today engines must be changed in some places where bridges still can not take the weight of an entire train. ▷

62

64

64.   *The Military Museum at Ben Luc,*
one of many founded all over the
country exhibiting American military
equipment captured by the Hanoi army
and used as long as in working
condition.

65.   War scrap has even been used for 'carousels' like the one in the picture. The 'plane' is an old auxiliary fuel tank extracted from the remains of an American aircraft.

66.   Cockpit of a Cessna A-37. During the war U.S. forces lost 3720 combat planes and 4865 helicopters. The Vietnamese adventure cost the U.S.A. around 300,000 million dollars, according to estimates made in 1974.

67

67. *The Viet Cong and North Vietnamese military cemetery in Bien Hoc. The list of Communists killed in combat is still incomplete. The number of casualties recorded up to 1974 (a year before the end of the war) was around 900,000 dead and 500,000 missing.*

68-71. *Vengeance in postwar times was not confined to the living: in the military cemetery in Saigon, graves were violated and headstones served as shooting targets. The number of South Vietnamese soldiers recorded as killed in action was 184,000, but statistics were not kept after 1973. The total of civilians who died in the war has been estimated at around one million.*

69

70

71

Economic Issues

NORTH AND SOUTH

Vietnam has the makings of a prosperous modern economy. Its resources might be envied by some countries whose economic performance has been better. The Vietnamese people are literate and industrious. The country is advantageously positioned in its region. The long coastline contains excellent harbors and provides access to the fruits of the sea at countless points. The lay of the land offers many different ways of exploiting the soil and space for farming and industry, and large expanses of land remain to be developed and tilled. Good soils are already in place for growing valuable forests. The varied mineral deposits include anthracite coal, and reports indicate sizable finds of oil and gas off the coasts. Finally, it has many rivers worth harnessing for electricity.

So why has there been so little visible progress after fifteen years of rule by a Communist party dedicated to economic development? Why is Vietnam still one of the poorest countries in the world?

Certainly the difficulties the leadership faced in 1975 were daunting in the short range. North Vietnam's victory in 1975 came a year or two sooner than it expected, obliging it to tackle difficult problems without full preparation. The flip-flop on the pace of economic integration — a momentous issue — suggested that some of the thinking and decisions were rushed. Second, withdrawal of the abundant aid that had been pumped into the two economies during the period of separation (1954-1975) — from China and the Soviet Union to the DRV and from the U.S. to South Vietnam — had a withering effect at both ends of the country. Third, the southern cities, especially Saigon, were in disastrous shape. They were so overpopulated people could not even be fed, much less housed, employed, educated, and treated for illness. Last, but still important, the country had not been bombed back into the proverbial Stone Age, but, short of using nuclear weapons, the 850,000 tons of bombs dropped on the North alone represented a fair attempt.

For some weeks after the fall of Saigon the strategy was to gradually merge the two economies in the course of the Second Five-Year Plan (1976-1980). Socialist institutions would be created in the South as economic development rolled along. Within weeks,

72. *Two small boys on top of a derelict American tank. According to Vietnamese statistics, the war left around 800,000 children without families, the majority of them orphans or the offspring of Euro-Asian or Afro-Asian unions, abandoned by their fathers, and sometimes their mothers.*

however, security considerations prevailed with a leadership formed in military campaigns that had lasted generations, and in August 1975 the decision was made to bring the two economies together by forcing the South into the austere model established in the North.

Two assumptions behind the decision to force the northern model on the South have not proved out. The first was that the northern economic model was viable and effective. The second was that the North's austere socialist model, even if sound, could be quickly imposed on the South, whose economy and people had been shaped for two centuries by a different economic and social way of life.

Unsuccessful attempts to assimilate a large capitalist region into its twenty-year-old socialist system has been Vietnam's economic story in the last fifteen years. Even as the leaders faced it in 1975, the South had different problems from the North. Its economy was largely based on free enterprise, there was less industry but a more important commercial sector, and the standard of living, given the far less dense population, was higher. The failure to transform the South in the North's image caused an economic and political crisis in 1979 which produced the first of several increasingly determined and far-reaching thrusts for reform in which leaders from the South became more prominent.

AGRICULTURE

An abundance of rice is the first condition of a normal economy in Vietnam. Yet rice production went into decline in 1976. There were technical reasons such as the weather and shortages of fertilizer, pesticides, gasoline, credit and spare parts for irrigation pumps, all of them required to grow the high-yield rice varieties adopted in the Sixties. The nontechnical reasons were the resistance of the southern farmers to collectivization and their refusal to produce a surplus for the market when money and consumer goods were so short.

The latter half of the Seventies saw the value of crop production bobbing up and down: up 10 percent in 1976, down five percent in 1977 when there was a drought, and no better in 1978 when major typhoons occurred and widespread flooding cut back livestock herds severely. The government responded by giving farmers greater incentives in 1978 and 1979. A contract system was supposed to guarantee them access to production supplies, but bureaucratic inefficiencies and shortages dashed hope for achieving food self-sufficiency by 1980, and the rice target was lowered from 21 to 15 million tons. Even that was not achieved.

The Third Five-Year Plan (1980-85) did little to brighten the picture. Food grain production grew faster than population, but in a country that must develop mining and industry with capital generated in agriculture, this could do no more than lift per capita food consumption a small notch. In 1986 farm families were spending four dong out of every five they earned on food. Two-thirds of the country's workforce was in agriculture, more than in 1976 and 1980.

When Vo Van Kiet, an economic reformer from the South, took over the planning ministry in 1986, he summed up the situation in agriculture. Fisheries and forestry had shown gains, but they represented only one-fifth of the sector. The farming branches making up the remainder had all fallen short of targets. Production of food crops other than rice was declining. Livestock output was up, meeting or exceeding planners expectations, but prices were unstable, and the supply of animal feed, a commodity entirely in government hands, was short. Kiet put the blame on government ministries and commissions, including his own, suggesting policy changes and a general shakeup, but the system itself was not questioned.

INDUSTRY

When the Democratic Republic of Vietnam (DRV) was created in 1954, its industry showed only minor evidence of modernity even though the North was the region endowed with industrial potential and even though France, a European power with an advanced economy, had held it for eighty years. Only a few thousand people were working in industry, which produced less than two percent of physical output. That industry consisted of the Nam Dinh yarn and textile mills, the Haiphong cement plant, the Hon Gay coal fields, and some breweries and cigarette factories. This changed quickly. By 1960 industry was producing 18 percent of the national income and employing seven percent of the labor force.

The first order of business in the postwar strategy for industry was to reassemble the northern factories and workshops dispersed to avoid bombardment and extend the power of the state over whatever sizable factories the South possessed. For a time industry displayed a certain vigor, but as resources were diverted to the new war effort in Cambodia and to defense of the northern border, shortages became more severe and bottlenecks more constricted. The invasion of Cambodia nipped in the bud good intentions of many multinational groups and Western countries to aid Vietnam after the country was re-united. The Chinese incursion, shallow as it was, penetrated deep enough to do severe damage to important towns, industrial plants and rail facilities. Industrial output grew negligibly between 1976 and 1980, the period of the Second Five-Year Plan. Relative to population, which was growing inexorably at better than two percent annually, it declined.

A certain price was paid for the ideological bias toward heavy industry. One difficulty of large-scale projects, which by definition take longer to build and show a return, was that under Vietnamese conditions the construction proper had to wait upon earthmoving done by hand. Light industry and handicrafts could do no better than the agriculture they depended on for raw materials. They peaked in 1978, then dipped below the output for 1976. As shortages of food and consumer goods intensified, workers had less and less reason to concentrate on their jobs and more and more reason to focus on other ways of feeding themselves and their families.

The best industrial growth during the third Five-Year Plan (1981-1985) was in paper production, thanks to a Swedish paper mill north of Hanoi, and food processing, a sector in which Soviet aid had been significant. Refined sugar production exceeded the 1975 level tenfold, and by 1985 ocean fish processing had returned to the 1975 level in spite of a unique difficulty: people had fled the country in so many fishing boats they had depleted the fleet. By 1985 light industry had scratched and clawed its way back to 1976 levels, and textile production was up. More electric power was being generated, but not enough: power shortages were holding back other sectors. Three large Soviet-aided power projects promise to ease the situation when they go on line at full capacity.

The Third Five-Year Plan committed over half of investments to industry and nearly one-fifth to agriculture, yet food production increased only 19.5 percent between 1980 and 1984. Emphasis was shifted from large-scale to small-scale industry. There were still some private operators left in the early Eighties, but most of the small plants operated as joint state-private companies or as cooperatives.

The Fourth Five-Year Plan (1986-1990) aimed at growth in three areas: food, consumer goods and exports. It included land-use, conservation and irrigation projects along the Mekong, dike repairs on the Red River, and fertilizer imports, and its emphasized pest control, tractor use, animal husbandry and seed production.

TRANSPORTATION

In the Eighties the Vietnamese economy was still hampered by a transportation system that had always been underdeveloped and was the segment of the economy's infrastructure most ravaged by the war.

The figures for the country's rail system are disheartening. In 1965 it carried 4.5 million tons of freight. Fifteen years later it carried one million tons less. If the length of the haul is taken into account, the results were better in 1980, but only slightly. Trucking is probably even worse off than rail transportation. Goods move slowly on a crowded highway with a 25-mile speed limit and with people drying rice on the edge of the roadway. The merchant fleet has been upgraded with Soviet assistance, and a major effort has been made to improve the seaports of Haiphong, Ho Chi Minh City and Danang, the country's largest, but they continue to be a weak link in an already inadequate transportation system.

Yet there are signs of modernization. In 1985 a pipeline to carry oil from the coastal city of Vinh to Vientiane, the capital of Laos, was completed to the Laotian border. Aeroflot and Air France provide international service to Hanoi's Noi Bai and Ho Chi Minh City's Tan Son Nhut airports, and Air Vietnam maintains regular air service between these cities and major Vietnamese towns and islands.

MONEY MATTERS

In addition to controlling the currency (the dong), credit, interest rates and other customary functions of a central bank, the State Bank of Vietnam conducts some of the operations of a commercial bank through its headquarters in Hanoi, a division in Ho Chi Minh City, and numerous provincial branches.

The finance ministry and the state bank put their heads together to draw up the state budget. This is quite a job, since this budget is the fountain from which all good things flow — not only for the central government, but also for 38 provincial and more than 500 local governments. Only one-third of the budget's revenues come from taxes. As the owner of the enterprises in the economy, the state collects the lion's share of their profits. In the 1980s it was not government practice to publish or release figures on the budget.

A mismanaged monetary reform plan set an inflationary blaze in 1985. The rate of inflation rose from 50 percent in 1985 to 700 percent by September 1986. The government fought back by using its fiat to lower prices. Price subsidies were re-introduced, and essential goods were once again rationed in the face of widespread shortages and hoarding. Changes in 1985 for the first time based wages on work done and established payment entirely in money, not partly or entirely in kind.

Outside experts agree that Vietnam's intricate pricing system has made other problems worse than they might otherwise have been. The state, set up as the sole buyer and sole reseller, paid one price for goods produced up to the target it assigned and another for goods produced over and above that amount. And then there were free market prices, generally higher. One reason state enterprises keep large amounts of cash on hand is that frequently they have to pay those prices for things they need to keep operating. Another is that the banks are readier to accept deposits than to honor withdrawals.

FOREIGN TRADE AND INVESTMENT

In 1975 government control was immediately established over foreign trade, but in 1981 the wave of reform initiated in 1979 relaxed the tight grip of the central authorities. The four cities with the most foreign dealings (Hanoi, Ho Chi Minh City, Haiphong and Danang) were allowed to set up import-export corporations so that the management of this sector could respond more quickly to opportunities, needs and adverse side-effects. One-fourth of proceeds from exports were left to the producers and local authorities — not, however, in the form of hard currency, but its equivalent of imported goods.

This effort in the early Eighties was set back in 1983 by Hanoi's desire to keep the South under closer economic and political control. This tug-of-war between the conflicting aims of promoting foreign trade and holding tight to this key sector reflects the crucial ambiguity in the leadership's approach to many problems, including private enterprise, peasant agriculture, and domestic commerce. In 1987 foreign trade was again loosened and decentralized.

The U.S. trade embargo and financial boycott imposed in May 1975 have enforced Vietnam's isolation within its region, but the SRV does have connections. For instance, it took up South Vietnam's membership in the Asian Development Bank and the International Monetary Fund. Between 1978 and 1986 Comecon (Council for Mutual Economic Assistance), the Communist economic community, became increasingly important in Vietnam's trade, and ties with Western nations and with non-Communist countries in the region weakened. The Soviet Union was by far its largest trading partner. As the Soviet economic situation has deteriorated, foreign aid cutbacks as large as 75 percent have been discussed. Vietnam will be severely affected.

In 1986 the Sixth Party Congress announced the target of a 70 percent growth of exports by 1990. Export incentives in effect manipulate the share of foreign-exchange earnings exporters are allowed to keep — both to encourage exports and to impose preferences on this sector. Firms in the highlands, exporters of rubber, coal and marine products, and the tourist industry are encouraged in this way.

Vietnam carries on some trade with other countries in Asia. Trade with Japan, said to be poised for lively business when Vietnam opens up, amounted to $285 million in 1986. Marine products and coal were exported, and imports were chemicals, textiles, machinery and transportation equipment. Vietnam imports chemicals, machinery and equipment, and industrial textiles from Hong Kong, while exports include prawns, plants used for perfume, and specialized animal products such as feathers. Singapore, an ASEAN nation, was expected to respect the boycott, yet its exports to Vietnam in 1985 were equal to those of Japan, and it imported twice as much from Vietnam as Hong Kong.

The U.S.S.R. is still Vietnam's largest trading partner. Soviet oil and petroleum products comprise one-third of the trade between the two countries. The U.S.S.R. is furnishing exploration equipment and technical aid against future recovery from finds, and in the meantime is meeting the economy's demand for petroleum products.

Vietnam has been more liberal toward foreign investors than other Communist countries in hopes of attracting capital through the fence set up by the financial boycott. The foreign investment law adopted in 1988 was heralded as the most liberal in Asia and stood out among those of Communist countries. It encourages joint ventures, allows wholly foreign-owned firms in Vietnam, envisages taxes of only 20-30 percent on profits, allows full repatriation of profits after taxes, and issues a guarantee against nationalization.

FOREIGN DEBT AND AID

In 1975 the U.S.S.R. cancelled Vietnam's debts in the amount of $450 million and began an aid program through outright grants. As Vietnam's trade with Comecon expanded, its debt continued to grow. Project assistance and related equipment financed by Comecon were wasted because of mismanagement or remained frozen for years in projects scheduled to produce in the mid-Eighties or later. Exports fell below targets, trade deficits widened, and additional help was needed to right the balance of payments. During the Third Five-Year Plan, the U.S.S.R. shifted to concessionary loans repayable at two percent interest over 20-30 years. In 1982 Vietnam defaulted on its international debts. While it exported $182 million to the non-Communist world, it owed $260 million in debt payments. In January 1985 the IMF suspended further credit. Talks to reschedule the $90-billion obligation broke down in 1987. That same year Vietnam owed $5.5-6 billion to Comecon countries and the total debt was about $1 billion to hard-currency creditors: the IMF, the Asian Development Bank, Belgium, Denmark, France, India, Japan, and the Netherlands. And finally it owed money to private investors in the West.

The $100 million in money orders which Vietnamese abroad send annually to Vietnam are important to many families' standard of living and to the country's finances. In addition, between $10 and $20 million are collected in customs duties on packages received from abroad.

Immediately following the fall of Saigon, Vietnam was receiving aid both from the West and the Soviet bloc to finance major development projects, to underwrite its fledgling export industries and to cover deficits in the balance of payments. Its ties became closer with the U.S.S.R. as the Cambodian invasion and border fight with China caused a sharp drop in aid from China, the West and international organizations.

Without aid from the Western countries Vietnam could not import their equipment. Sweden was the only Western country that continued its aid at that time. The Mekong River Development Project under United Nations auspices, originally adopted by multilateral agreement in 1957, did continue. The average annual amount of Western aid through 1986 was about $100 million. Meanwhile the deficit in current payments was $221 million. Hanoi had to rely very heavily on the Soviets, who provided abundant help in the resumption of oil explorations. The annual amount of Soviet aid was between $700 million and $1 billion.

REFORM

Agriculture has failed to produce surplus income to finance other sectors. Food production has in fact grown only just faster than population, and malnutrition was being mentioned in the late Eighties as one reason why productivity is so low. Another is the shortage of consumer goods — why work hard if there is nothing to buy with the extra money you will earn? Or perhaps the chance to earn more with extra work is not even there. Wages in the socialized firms are largely egalitarian, varying little up or down from the average. With food so scarce, workers look outside their regular workplace for ways to feed their families.

Low productivity is just one of the ways in which the policies of the leadership in Hanoi have diverted, disabled or discarded human resources indispensable to the economy. The imprisonment of entire categories of citizens without charges or trials and the use of the resettlement program as a security instrument deprived the economy of a large number of people with abilities to offer. It turned many potential friends of the regime into enemies. The huge military establishment diverted people from what they might have contributed to economic development projects: rebuilding the war-damaged roads, railroad lines, dikes, irrigation and bridges. The peremptory moves against the commercial sector drove from the country people with the entrepreneurial spirit and initiative every Communist country is now looking for. The effort to pressure a viable agriculture into accepting organizational forms that have not worked effectively elsewhere stifled the country's main resource: the millions of peasants whose lives are bound to the soil.

In the 1980s the trend was toward greater price flexibility, but prices of both production supplies and consumer goods were set by the government on the basis of average standard costs, taxes and an assigned rate of profit. In April 1987 a policy of rational prices based on costs and projected consumer demand was put into place for industry.

Now the leaders are looking for solutions to institutions long familiar in the South, just as *perestroika* has Communist leaders almost everywhere looking to the capitalist system for answers to their difficulties. Hindsight, sharpened by what has happened to other Communist systems, suggests the value of an open-minded rivalry between the two economies to explore the virtues and defects of each in solving Vietnam's unique problems. It seems a pity that history did not allow that option fifteen years ago. It will take a brilliant leadership to referee it even now.

75. Cockfight in a Saigon street. People place bets and enjoy themselves during these fights, which are popular throughout Asia. In small villages, they become important social events.

74, 76. The village market is such an integral part of everyday life that not even the horrors of war could completely interrupt its existence. During the war it served not only for small-scale commerce, but as a front for entirely different activities, such as the illegal purchase of arms, exchange of vital information, and a hiding place for those in danger.

77

77. A seemingly well-supplied shop in Ho Chi Minh City, at one time an unusual sight in the former capital of the South. Despite all its wartime sufferings and the period of 're-education' imposed on it, the city continues to be richer and happier than Hanoi.

78. Bookstore in Hanoi. Notwithstanding the limitations imposed by shortage of paper, the inhabitants of the capital are voracious readers, with a preference for romantic novels.

79.   An itinerant woman vendor at the black market in Cholon, former stronghold of the Chinese merchant class in Saigon. This market has managed to survive under the new regime. During the U.S. involvement, it was even better supplied, via the PX, supposedly reserved for American forces.

80.   Wide-brimmed straw hats protect the Vietnamese peasants against sun and rain, and in the case of women, from indiscreet glances. In the North, the men replaced this attractive headwear with colonial-style pith helmets. ▷

81, 82.   Soccer is Vietnam's favorite sport. Players on the bench of the Da Nang team watch the game. In the interval, the public, referee and linesmen focus on my camera. I discovered that the local soccer fans knew the names of every player in the Italian national team.

82

83.   The team's goalkeeper poses proudly, in spite of the number of goals he conceded.

84.   Players taking a break at half-time. It is strange that even in this extremely poor country, players wear boots of the finest quality. One pair costs the equivalent of two high monthly salaries. In relative terms, soccer seems to be as profitable in Vietnam as in Western countries.

84

85-87. *Village funeral near Haiphong.* 85
*Judging by the crowd, the deceased must
have been an important or well-loved
person. A funeral does not appear to be
a mournful occasion in Vietnam. The
long procession of those attending is
accompanied by music and flags.
Children carry the flags, men in the
prime of life carry the coffin, and old
men chant laments all the way to the
cemetery.*

88. *A young peasant girl, showing a
certain coyness in the presence of my
camera, protects herself from the rain
with two baskets as an improvised hat.* ▷

86

89. *Woman in traditional Vietnamese
dress admiring the decorated columns of
the Imperial Palace in Hué, residence of
monarchs from 1802 until 1945.* ▷ ▷

130

95

95. *Entrance to a Montagnard house. The French called the ethnic minorities 'Montagnards' because they mostly inhabit the mountainous zone of the interior. Some were already in place there at the dawn of history, while others were pushed into the highlands by Viet expansion.*

96. *Hut of wood, bamboo and straw* *belonging to a Montagnard tribal chief,* *near Ban Me Thuot. The villages are* *small, consisting of no more than a* *dozen huts, each housing 8-10 people.*

96

99. Broken windshield of a city bus in Ho Chi Minh City. ▷

100. This ancient army vehicle converted into a minibus painfully hauls itself up the Pleiku road, while the passengers follow on foot to help it. For adaptation to civilian life, many such vehicles had to be converted from gasoline to coal. ▷ ▷

101. Confirmation that the Vietnamese distrust every other means of transport but the bicycle: even when traveling by bus, they carry them fastened to the roof. The bicycle is used for the last leg of their trip, somewhere off the main road, and is also a backup in case the bus breaks down. ▷ ▷ ▷

97

97. The Vietnamese railroad system is outdated and inadequate. There is only one railroad running along the coast between Hanoi and the former Saigon, and the trains keep no schedule. Freight has to be loaded by hand, since there is no mechanization.

98. The stationmistress controls traffic on the Dan Rong railroad bridge, a few miles north of Quang Tri. An important strategic point, it was severely damaged by bombing and had to be rebuilt after the war.

45A·70·58

143

102

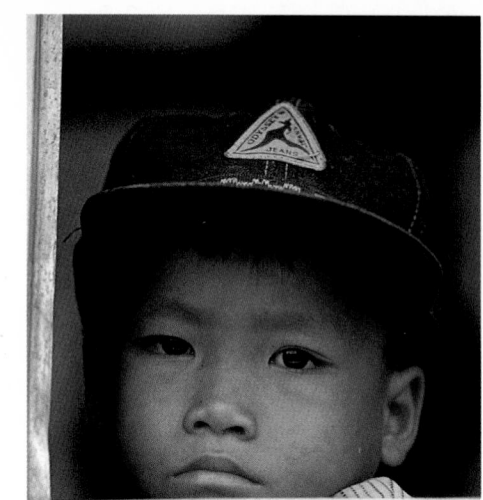

102. *Serious, inquiring look from a small boy, his face framed in a bus window.*

103. *An American car now turned into a taxi-bus. It makes its rounds between villages and markets carrying everything and everyone, getting the job done in any way it can.*

103

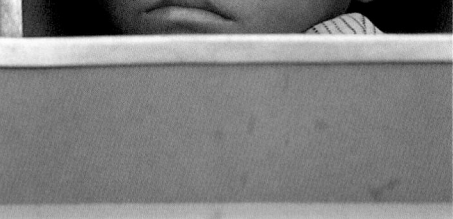

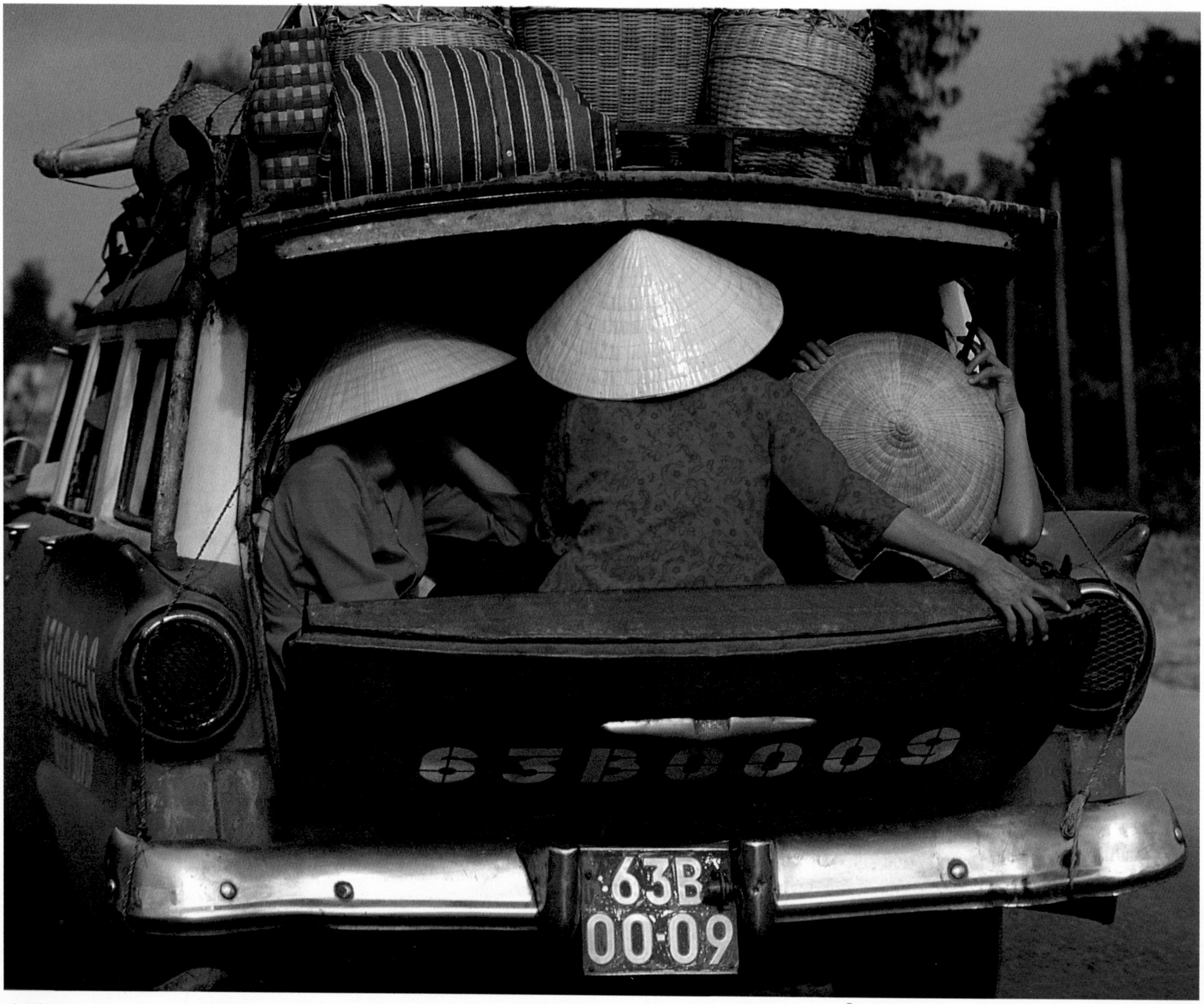

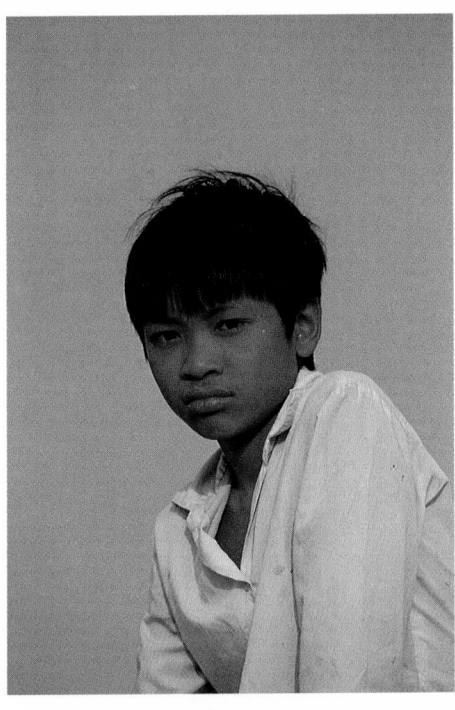

104, 105. *Vietnamese boy, and a baby pressed between its mother's back and the bus seat. Children are both the greatest hope and tragedy of Vietnam, a country of 66 million people with a great demographic problem. About 4500 new inhabitants are born every day. The average age of married couples is low (20-23), and nearly all wish to have at least one male child.*

105

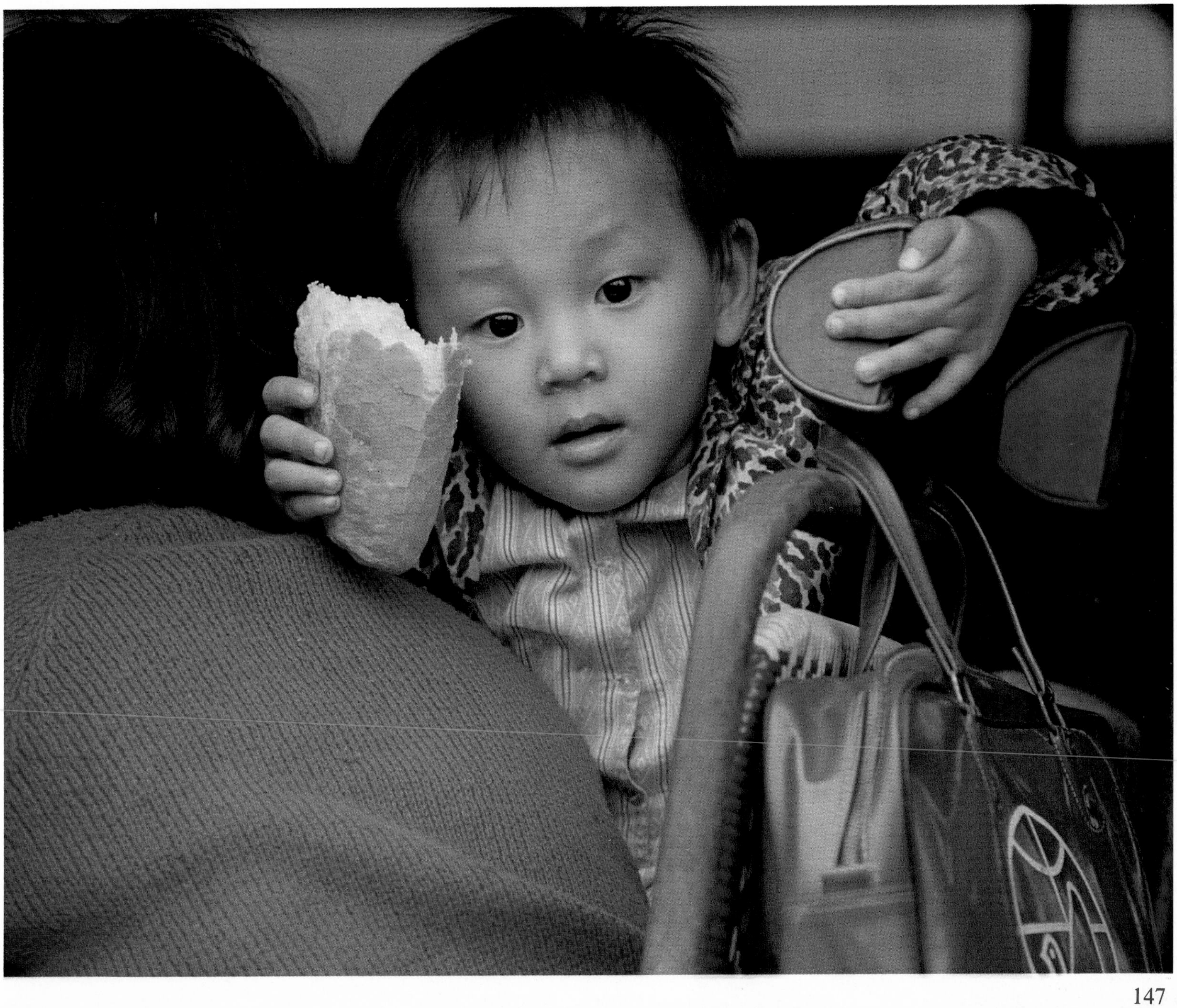

147

106

106. *Vehicles are constantly breaking down. The truck in this picture was standing there when I drove past. Two days later I found it in the same spot, along with all its passengers and the driver-mechanic.*

107.   *A traveling salesman pedals away,
half-buried by his goods. The bicycle is
invaluable in Vietnam. During festivities
it serves to take whole families for a
ride. Generally, every family owns one,
while the better-off have two or three.* ▷

World War II, he adopted the peasant's pajamas as his costume; later, as president of the DVR, he lived at the French governor-general's residence — in the gardener's cottage, where he tended his own garden. Perhaps that modesty was a kind of discipline. As a statesman he was always negotiating from a weak position, always the 'grasshopper among the elephants'. The tactic of 'talking and fighting, fighting and talking' was imposed. In 1946, for example, he signed the agreement assenting to the French Union in the face of deep disappointment in his own party. No one knew better than he that the French were offering the same domination done up in a new package, meant only to satisfy the form, not the substance, of American anti-colonial sensitivities. But he signed because he had both the Chinese and the French sitting in Tonkin and lacked the strength to settle them both at once. A stroke of the pen dropped the Chinese from the equation. Meanwhile, General Giap was already knee-deep in preparations to fight the French.

THE PARTY

Ho's role in the founding of the Indochinese Communist Party set the pattern of his leadership until his death. In his absence the Thanh Nien (Revolutionary Youth) dissolved into northern and southern factions, whereupon both set themselves up as Communist parties. The Tan Viet, a rival of the Thanh Nien, formed a third. The Comintern (Communist International), the organization through which Moscow tried to guide the world Communist movement, sent its circuit rider in Asia, Ho Chi Minh, to deal with these factions in the role of Dutch uncle. In late January 1930 he went from Thailand to Hong Kong and summoned two representatives from each of the Thanh Nien groups. Meeting in the stands during a soccer game on February 3, they agreed to a reconciliation around the new program Ho proposed. He then dispatched them to bring the Tan Viet group into the fold. The Vietnamese Communist Party was created at the end of the month, but in October changed its name to the Indochinese Communist Party (ICP).

The party which Ho cemented together from factions in the movement had many lines of potential division in its later history: hard-liners versus moderates, pro-Beijing versus pro-Moscow, proponents of DRV development (prior to 1959) versus extension of control over South Vietnam, pragmatists versus ideologues, proponents of all-out war versus a protracted combination of military and propaganda efforts to win South Vietnam, and, within the military, advocates of big-unit war versus proponents of a fifty-year war of attrition. How did a party so divided display such exemplary solidarity over the long period from the 1930s to the 1970s? One scholar suggests that the propensity to discord acted like a vaccine, and strong collective leadership was the response to contain the centrifugal forces. But the vaccine worked only while Ho was alive and while the war was going on. Various accounts mention divisions behind the scenes that date from the period of Ho's death, and since the end of the war several have been public.

The principal political project which the postwar leadership undertook has not materialized: the South has not been transformed in imitation of the socialist North. The brand of socialism taken as a model has repeatedly proved to be inefficient in agriculture and in the industrial workplace. Neither sector has been productive or profitable except in the periods when this obstinate effort was relaxed. Bent on an orthodox socialization of the South, they allowed the economy to jam up completely.

CONSTITUTION AND GOVERNMENT

Communist regimes regularly scrap constitutions every few years; it is a way of changing gears. The SRV adopted its third in 1980. Article 4 sets the tone when it declares the party to be "the vanguard and general staff of the Vietnamese working class", "the only force leading the state and society" and "the main factor determining all successes of the Vietnamese revolution". The first constitution, adopted in 1946, was part of the bid for legitimacy and a broad base at a time when the Viet Minh was not advertising its Communist inspiration. The standard Communist constitution adopted in 1959 coincided with the effort to take over the South by military means. It set up a parliamentary structure, but the real power remained with the VCP Political Bureau. The 1980 constitution was motivated by the reunification of North and South. It stated the goal of the Three Revolutions (in production relations, science and technology, and culture and ideology), called for a fresh start, and was highly Soviet-oriented. A thorough rewrite is currently underway to accommodate the fundamental changes occurring in economic life and to point directions for political life in the age of *perestroika*.

The National Assembly is a parliament responsible for adopting constitutions and laws and for approving state plans and budgets. In formal terms the supreme body of government, its actual function is to rubber-stamp documents implementing the policy of the Politbureau of the VCP. Deputies are elected to five-year terms through party-engineered elections. In recent years the candidates have been more varied, and debate has ranged more widely.

The 1980 constitution created the Council of State as a collective presidency with both legislative and executive authority, but it has less power than the Council of Ministers, which executes policy handed down by the party.

The French administered the territory of present-day Vietnam in the three regions of Tonkin, Annam and Cochinchina. Hanoi chose to eliminate the regional level of administration, which would have given the central and southern regions a formal government and a status equivalent to that of the northern region. It also set the largest cities apart from their respective regions by giving them the status of autonomous municipalities. They and the 36 provinces are administered directly from Hanoi.

SOCIAL OVERSIGHT AND LAW ENFORCEMENT

The postwar regime had no qualms about incarcerating anyone who might be at all dangerous to its security. It also kept a watchful eye on those still in circulation. One way it did this was through the warden system. Every hamlet, city block, state farm, workplace, school, and state and party office has its own watchdog committee headed by a warden. The committee is large enough to include many ordinary members drawn from the various parts of the community which the committee is set up to monitor. By the late 1980s there were signs that this system was not working as well as before. A second method of keeping tabs is through the party apparatus, which even without the warden network would still be a spider web extending into every hamlet, apartment building, workplace and school. Finally, there is the system of identity cards and family registration certificates.

Under the 1985 criminal code four groups of agencies were responsible for preventing crime and maintaining public order and internal security: the People's Security Force or People's Police, which was mainly urban; the People's Public Security Force or People's Security Service at the village level; the plainclothes or secret police; and the People's Armed Security Force, a quasi-military organization seeded with personnel from the regular military, operating mainly in villages and rural areas to combat both ordinary crime and activities mounted against the state.

The system of regular courts consists of the Supreme People's Court at the top of the pyramid and courts similarly organized at the province, district and city levels. There is also a military system of tribunals. No effort has been made to free the court system of party influence; the courts thus function as an expression of unquestioned authority, and the appeal system is little used.

RE-EDUCATION AND RESETTLEMENT

There is no question that the regime felt its position uncertain enough in the South to justify placing the highest priority on security. The re-education camps were not only separate from the New Economic Zones (NEZs), they were also set apart from the regular prison system. People were sent to the re-education camps not because of any crime they had committed, but because they were visible representatives of the old order. There were three types of camp. The short-term or minimum-security camp had two categories of inmates: those sentenced to 30 days' confinement and those given terms of three to six months. You could not expect to return from the long-term camp sooner than in half a year, and the longest term was three years. Anyone committed to the permanent camp had a fair chance of not returning at all. For one thing, conditions were poor, there was little food and no medicine, and the death rate was high. For another, although the two levels of these camps were referred to as three-year and five-year camps, those original sentences were renewable indefinitely at the discretion of the authorities.

The re-education camps were an alternative to large-scale executions. Their purpose was the physical removal of all potential leaders in the South until the regime felt stable enough to tolerate their release. This group included educators, legislators, province chiefs, writers and supreme court judges. In 1987 at least 15,000 were still imprisoned in the permanent camps, but by 1990 their remaining inmates were released or scheduled for release under an agreement whereby they would emigrate to the United States.

Resettlement is a drastic solution to a drastic problem of overpopulation. This major political issue is usually associated with the crowded northern delta. But that problem had been centuries in the making and therefore was not without its accommodations. In 1976 the leaders faced a much more acute and short-term problem of overcrowding in the southern cities, which had become bloated by the war effort that floated prosperously on American aid. Food shortages and unemployment compounded the problem of urban overcrowding. A keenly security-conscious leadership inevitably saw millions of hungry, homeless and jobless citydwellers as an incendiary political hazard.

The ultimate goal of resettlement set in 1976 was to move 10 million people over twenty years and achieve a relatively uniform distribution of population throughout the country's 443 districts with an average of 200,000 persons in each district living on 200,000 hectares. In a country with such extreme differences in terrain and where population patterns over millennia had been extremely onesided, this was a social engineering project of immense magnitude. Perhaps only a leadership that had already accomplished 'miracles' on the battlefield could have conceived and seriously contemplated such a scheme.

Large migrations did occur. In 1975 and 1976 more than 600,000 people were moved out of Ho Chi Minh City to New Economic Zones (NEZs). In the early going many fled the primitive camps that had been hastily set up and returned to the familiar if depressingly unpromising situation in the city. Some continued their flight and formed one of the sources of the stream of 'boat people'. When the military and youth organizations effectively tackled the task of camp development, not so many people felt that they had been sent to penal institutions, and the returnee rate dropped off sharply. Economic reform measures that began in 1979 have also helped make life in the zones more attractive to their inhabitants.

During the first five years after the war four million people were moved to rural areas. In the 1981-1985 period another two million people moved out of the cities, reducing the share of the cities in the total population from 19.3 percent in 1979 to 18 percent in 1985.

Although the NEZs were quite separate from the re-education camps, the sense that relocation was a punishment was not altogether off the mark. The public rationale for redistribution of population was economic, but since the NEZs soon got a bad name, the authorities were able to use the threat of relocation as a disguised and indirect instrument for coercing people.

POLICY TOWARD TRIBAL PEOPLES

Resettlement programs inevitably look to Vietnam's sparsely settled uplands, comprising 80 percent of the country's area, as one of their targets. This imperative compounds the inherent problem of population groups whose ways depart so radically from the general direction of the country and whose slash-and-burn agriculture is so wasteful of natural and human resources.

The Communists have a history of close relations with the tribal minorities. During the First Indochina War the Viet Minh relied heavily on support from mountain tribemen. After taking power in the North, it showed sensitivity for the Montagnard fear of domination by the Viet majority, establishing separate administration of the tribal uplands by party cadres who came from that environment. An effort was made to introduce some settlements to sedentary agriculture for the first time, but a way of life that had held its own for thousands of years was treated with kid gloves.

Saigon was meanwhile governing the tribal uplands with a heavy hand. Diem had alienated the Montagnards by settling Catholic refugees from the North on tribal lands. The Jarai and Rhade tribes displaced in that move remained backbones of rebellion long afterward. President Thieu allowed the tribal peoples some autonomy, but then drove them into the arms of the NLF with the Strategic Hamlet Program. FULRO (*Front Unifié de la Lutte des Races Opprimées*) was formed in 1964 to represent the Bahnar, Cham, Ede (Rhade), Hre, Jarai, Mnong, Raglai, Sadang, Stieng and other tribes.

The handling of the tribal peoples in the South immediately after the war contrasted sharply with the treatment given their northern counterparts during and after the First Indochina War. One reason was the unexpected early end of the Second Indochina War. After Dien Bien Phu the job had been given to trained party people who had come out of the tribes. This time military commanders at the local level had to handle issues that went beyond their training. In time the government did send people down, and in 1977 it set up the university at Buon Me Thuot to train native cadres.

In the mid-Eighties the party and the media declared satisfaction with the results in forming cooperatives and the trend toward sedentary farming. In 1986, they claimed, 43 percent of the 2.2 million members of the minorities practicing shifting agriculture had become sedentary. Viets were being moved into the uplands in ever greater numbers. But progress was actually spotty. The ingrained Vietnamese bias against the tribal minorities has not disappeared, nor has tribal suspicion of Vietnamese intentions. The SRV has even faced armed opposition from the tribes. FULRO was revived in 1979 when tribal unrest was renewed. Battles occurred involving as many as 1000 rebel fighters, whose general aim has not been to overthrow the regime, but just to be left alone. In 1987, a year in which ethnic minorities held 14 percent of the seats in the National Assembly, some local accommodation seemed to have been achieved.

FOREIGN RELATIONS

The Vietnamese outlook after 1975 sacrificed communication and trade to a strongly held posture. Vietnam's leadership has been willing to accept isolation and other high costs for its policies.

The 1979 the Chinese 'punitive' invasion was a spinoff of the Cambodian conflict, but China and Vietnam have differences apart from Cambodia and apart from any third country. Historically, when China did not actually rule its small southern neighbor, it expected compliance when it put its foot down. Communism does not seem to have changed that situation.

When and how Vietnam and China will work out a new mode of relations remain open questions. China still supports the Khmer Rouge in Cambodia and rebellious unrest of the tribal minorities. Conflicting territorial claims in the South China Sea involve potential oil discoveries. Yet against the background of shrinking Soviet aid and Soviet overtures to the Chinese, there were small signs in late 1990 that Vietnam and China might try to patch up their differences.

Relations with the Americans seem to be improving. In the spring of 1990 several public figures in the United States expressed strong criticism of two elements of the country's policy in Southeast Asia.

The Soviet model can be seen in Vietnam's constitution and its government institutions and management structures. In the 1980s the U.S.S.R. extended its already substantial involvement in the education sector. The twenty-five-year Treaty of Friendship and Cooperation between the two countries has run half its course, but the events of the last five years within the Soviet Union and the disastrous deterioration of the Soviet economy as the Nineties opened must place a question mark over the magnitude of future Soviet assistance.

110

110. *Crowd at a soccer match at Da Nang stadium. Sports are one of the few ways to release the tension that results from an arduous existence. Life is especially hard in the South, where Communist rule has not made poverty any easier to bear.*

111.   *A long line of visitors waits patiently for hours on end to pay their respects to the earthly remains of 'Uncle Ho'. Amid growing dissatisfaction with the regime, Ho Chi Minh's immense personal popularity has remained unassailed.*

112.   *A delegation from the Philippines, escorted by a Vietnamese official, at Ho Chi Minh's mausoleum. The ceremonial is very rigid, and once inside the tomb one is obliged to remain silent. Ho wanted his body cremated, but the leadership overrode his wishes.*

112

113, 114.   Entrance to the mausoleum
where the embalmed body of Ho Chi
Minh lies in state. He founded the
Vietnamese Communist Party in 1930 and
was the first head of the Democratic
Republic of Vietnam. He died in 1969, at
114   the age of 80.

115.   The enormous marble and granite
mausoleum of Ho Chi Minh close to Ba
Dinh Square. Completed on September 2,
1975, it was built with the help of the
Soviet Union and contributions in
material from the population of Vietnam.

118

116

116-119.   *A young policeman and three soldiers. The great variety of uniforms and headgear reflects the organizational structure, which consists of different types and ranks of militia and police that vary from region to region.*

120.   *General Tran Back (opposite) was commander of all Viet Cong forces in Saigon. He led his men through 10,000 days of war, driving around in a black Mercedes from his headquarters in central Saigon to clandestine command posts scattered throughout the city. He now devotes his retirement to writing books and giving interviews.*

119

121. *A group of youngsters posing under a government propaganda display. The party is constantly accusing this first postwar generation of capitalist ways, of becoming egoistic and arrogant toward their elders, and of lacking the capacity for self-sacrifice so deeply ingrained in their fathers and grandfathers.* ◁ ◁

122. *Teacher and pupils in front of Ho Chi Minh's bust during a school ceremony in the city that now bears his name. Vietnam is a young country governed by politicians who are mostly in their late seventies.* ◁

CHIẾN THẮNG ẤP BẮC.2

123, 124. Political propaganda posters in Bien Hoc. The reunification of North and South did not eliminate political and ideological differences between the two parts of the country. The poster above commemorates a battle with U.S. forces at the village of Ap Bac in the Mekong Delta.

125. Vietnamese schoolchildren find my camera irresistible. Westerners always attract children's attention since they are a rare sight (apart from Russians). The government has undertaken energetic measures to end illiteracy. ▷

GIỒNG DỨA

04 - 1947

Everyday Life

HOLIDAYS

Holidays tell a foreigner what a people treasures from its past. They also represent time set apart from the everyday round for deeper concerns of the spirit, the family, and the nation. Vietnam's traditional holidays are reckoned in the lunar or Chinese calendar.

The main religious holidays are Buddhist. On Buddha's Birthday in the fourth lunar month, Buddhists present offerings at pagodas, and lantern processions snake through the streets and entwine temples. Buddha's Illumination commemorates Buddha's ascent to Paradise on the eighth day of the twelfth month. In springtime pilgrims travel by small boat along canals past a succession of shrub-covered limestone prominences and climb on foot to the Buddhist Pagoda of Perfume in the Huong Son Mountains, less than 40 miles north of Hanoi.

Wandering Souls Day is celebrated in August. In a society so awed of ancestors, it is tragic not to bear sons to maintain the family altar and to carry on the line. Many holidays are occasions for cleaning graves and dressing altars, but this one is devoted to the souls of the dead who have no descendants to pray for them.

Seasonal celebrations include the mid-autumn festival celebrated on the eighth and largest full moon of the lunar year, which falls in late September. This has become a children's holiday with gift-giving, colorful dragon dances, and special foods. One moon later the coming of 'winter' is celebrated in the North with kite-flying.

Modern 'political' holidays begin on February 3 with the Founding of the Communist Party of Vietnam. In the late spring Liberation Day (the fall of Saigon in 1975 on April 30), International Workers Day (May Day), Dien Bien Phu Day a week later, and then Ho Chi Minh's Birthday (May 19) are clustered in close succession. National Day on September 2 commemorates Ho's reading of the Vietnamese Declaration of Independence in Hanoi on the day when the Japanese surrendered in 1945.

A few holidays are associated with legends. The Lac Long Quan Festival celebrates the dragon lord who came from his home in the sea to plant the seed of the Vietnamese people by marrying the Chinese immortal Au Co. He is credited with having brought rice culture to the Vietnamese. Their union produced 100 eggs from

126. Monument commemorating war victims. Such memorials can be found in nearly every place where a battle was fought or executions were carried out.

which 100 sons were hatched. The couple divided them equally and went their separate ways, she to the mountains and he to the lowlands. His oldest son, regarded as the true founder of the Hung dynasty and of the nation, is commemorated on Hung Vuong, which falls on the tenth day on the third month.

Tet takes up at least the first three days of the new lunar year. Spring comes early in a country with little or no winter, so Tet, once an agrarian festival, is a celebration of renewal, although it falls in late January or February, in between the first and second rice crops. Later it spread to the city and became the country's most important public holiday of the year. More than a holiday, Tet is an annual festival, a celebration of many reasons for living.

Preparations begin a week or more in advance. Booths set up in city streets sell boughs with peach or plum blossom to decorate the house – as obligatory to the Vietnamese as the Christmas tree in Christian countries. Marketplaces large and small are crowded to overflowing right up to the last day of the old year. Week-long processions send off the household hearth spirit to report to the Emperor of Jade on how things stand in the family. He returns in the last hour of the old year. Tet is another occasion to pay homage to ancestors, a time to pay off debts, and a fitting moment to turn over a new leaf, forgiving oneself and others for past mistakes.

Each day of the Tet celebration has its distinct purpose. The first day is set aside for the family, which gathers to greet the coming of spring on the eve of the new year. To start the new year right, a favorite friend is invited to be the first visitor in the morning. The second day celebrates friendship, and the third is traditionally devoted to village business, when the adult members of the village would gather in the *dinh* or communal hall to discuss plans for the next crop.

Aside from the universal firecrackers and holiday sweets, Tet is celebrated in different ways from place to place. In one village they might have cock fights, in another contests of musicians, drummers and dancers, tree planting, fencing with beribboned foils, sword-fights, boat races, puppet theater performances, tugs-of-war, singing and dancing accompanied by flute, drum and zither, theater performances until late into the night, martial arts demonstrations, crossbow shoots, choral performances, and folk dances in which revellers wielding shields, hats, umbrellas, poles or cudgels wind around a stake or jug of wine.

The Tet feast in Vietnamese families includes all the specialties of the national cuisine, but the most important dish on the table is the *banh chung*, a kind of meat and bean pie wrapped in a banana leaf. A farmer may tuck this neat and nourishing package into his bib when he sets out at dawn to work all day in distant fields.

FOOD AND CLOTHING

In the uplands of Vietnam, which were long ignored by both

the Chinese and Vietnamese in the plains, the spread of Chinese influence can be traced by the transition from chopsticks to the Southeast Asian style of eating with the fingers. While Southeast Asians typically blend their rice with other ingredients in cooked dishes, the Chinese and Vietnamese like their rice separate.

Just as the Vietnamese used Chinese characters for so many centuries without adopting Chinese as their language, so their use of chopsticks has not made their cooking Chinese. The distinctiveness of Vietnamese cooking after a thousand-year occupation by a country with one of the world's great cuisines is more small evidence that the Vietnamese cultural identity was formed before the Chinese came south and discovered them two thousand years ago.

Stir-frying is done in the kitchens of both countries, but Vietnamese cooks stir with extra-long chopsticks instead of the Chinese spatula. They prefer simmering and do much less deep-frying than the Chinese. Vietnamese food, known for its lightness, makes far less use of oil and thickeners like cornstarch. Health-conscious devotees of the *nouvelle cuisine* have become its supporters. The yeoman's work of soy sauce in Chinese cooking is done by *nuoc mam* or fish sauce, a feature of Southeast Asian cooking, as is the liking for the sweet or sticky type of rice.

Fish sauce is made from anchovies salted down and fermented in barrels for half a year. *Nuoc mam* is so fundamental to the Vietnamese diet that there are factories making it in Vung Tau and many other coastal towns, where both the salt and fish are taken directly from the sea.

The Vietnamese household does its cooking with charcoal over a small stove made of clay, which is always kept on the kitchen floor. The food is grilled rather than baked. Another smaller clay stove is used at the table. The mortar and pestle are in constant use in a Vietnamese kitchen, where the abundance of small pots and bowls reflects a cuisine based on blending many ingredients.

Diverse historical influences on the regions of Vietnam have given them different ways of preparing their food. The northerners come closest to the Chinese. Some of the spices and ingredients used in the South are not so ready to hand in the cooler climate of the North. Black pepper is used more than the red. Crabs are important in the northern diet, where less fish is eaten than in the South. The light and decorative touch of Vietnamese meals is characteristic of the central region, where people almost always include red chilis in their recipes. Some meals seem to be made entirely of prettily arranged garnishes. In the South the basic Vietnamese cuisine served in the North has been augmented with French and Indian influences.

The Vietnamese version of the loose shirt and trousers typical of tropical climates resembles 'pajamas' and is the universal peasant costume of men and women. Very young children go naked. The dressier *ao dai*, also tunic and trousers, can be very elegant on an older woman and graceful and alluring on a young woman. The long tunic has a deep slit, making flaps that flutter in the breeze. And many disparate pieces of long-wearing military clothing, too useful to throw away, are still in style.

Sandals of leather, rubber and plastic are the virtually universal footwear of those Vietnamese who are not barefoot in this tropical climate. Men wear hats of all kinds, many not tropical at all, like standard European berets, sometimes worn inside out. Pith helmets, some of them with a vintage patina, are very common, along with baseball caps, broad-brimmed straw and palm hats of the kind favored by tropical farmers worldwide, and military caps reminiscent of every army that has come this way. Women who do not wear the cone-hat may cover their head with a scarf, cloth or towel and knot it at the back. Some are thick and warm, others so thin as to resemble skullcaps. The conical reed-and-grass native hat is the most common head covering of men, women and children in both city and country. The landscape would not be the same without it: in any scene the white triangle is a magnet to the eye.

THE FAMILY

As one would expect in a society that experienced forty years of warfare within contemporary lifetimes, Vietnamese women outnumber the men by a few percentage points. War also has something to do with the young age of the population. Children and adolescents (under age twenty) constitute a majority. Life expectancy is in the early sixties for men and mid-sixties for women. This is a striking increase since 1960, when it was estimated at thirty-five.

The most remarkable and ultimately disturbing feature of the population is its growth. In the mid-Sixties the combined population of North and South Vietnam was 34 million. It was 66 million in the 1989 Census. The annual growth rate of 2.5 percent adds 1,625,000 people to the population every year. Vietnam is the world's twelfth most populous country. But the figure of 508 persons per square mile does not give the true picture, since the country's uplands, 80 per cent of its area, are still sparsely settled.

The traditional model of the Vietnamese family, that model overlaid on the Southeast-Asian pattern by the Confucianist outlook, incorporated the authoritarian social system. As the subject owed allegiance to the emperor, so the wife was to obey the husband, the family the father, the child the parent, the younger the older brother. The family member did not have interests that overrode those of the family as a whole. Moreover, in the context of the ancestor cult, the family was not confined to living members, but included those gone before and those yet unborn. Spirits of the deceased, it was thought, could influence their descendants' lives. Efforts to please ancestors began with care about where to bury them. After burial the eldest son took responsibility for maintaining graves and observing rites.

The family structure was patrilineal. The homestead passed to the eldest son, who brought his wife into the home when he married. Thus a four-generation household was common: grandparents, parents, their eldest son and his children. The extended family was the ideal, but the nuclear family was usually the reality. Marriages were arranged by contract between the parents in the family interest, and the participants were not to object. A man could have concubines or multiple wives. The second and third wife and their children would sometimes live in the home, sometimes elsewhere.

Perhaps it is the Southeast-Asian legacy of two virtually equal lines of parental authority in the Vietnamese family that accounts for the strong fiber of the women. They are tough and determined, they make good managers, they do the selling and much of the farm work, and they usually take care of the money. But women are under-represented in university enrollment, in the bureaucracy entered via the university, and in public life generally.

Equal roles for men and women in the family and equality for women in the workplace and in public life are Communist goals. Few social institutions have changed as much as the family since 1954. The 1959 DRV law on marriage and the family, extended to southern Vietnam in 1977, prohibited polygyny, concubinage and abuse. Women were allowed to choose their husband. The law's passage was backed up with a campaign of social pressure to discourage lavish wedding feasts, dowries and large families. The age suggested for marriage was twenty for men, eighteen for women, a good two years older than customary. Birth control lectures were given in the workplace, and a limit of two children per couple was recommended.

Yet some of the old traditions still persisted in the Eighties. The change was slower in rural and upland areas. The new law on marriage and the family passed in 1986 was another move to shape family attitudes in the national interest of a lower birth rate. The outlook for this is not promising when surveys show that most parents want at least three children and attach so much importance to a son. Perhaps there is promise in the desire of most parents to see their children leave farming.

In a Vietnamese name the family name comes first. Since there are only some 300 of these family names to provide handles for 65 million people, a second or middle name is included as a closer identifier. The personal name comes last, but this is the one to use in addressing someone formally. Nguyen Thanh To, for example, would be adressed as 'Mr. To'. Although his wife may keep her maiden name for professional reasons, she will ordinarily take her husband's family name, but she will be addressed not as 'Mrs. Nguyen', but as 'Mrs. To'.

HEALTH CARE

The steep climb of life expectancy in Vietnam from under age

181

thirty before World War II to about sixty at present testifies to how little was done earlier to prevent and treat the diseases that afflicted the population into the last quarter of this century. Nearly one-third of the population suffered from malaria; half suffered from trachoma, and 100,000 people were blind. Cholera outbreaks claimed tens of thousands of lives every few years. Between one and two percent of the population were infected with leprosy. The general mortality rate was one of the world's highest, and infant mortality was 30 per 1000. Even in 1945, 20 mothers in every 1000 died giving birth.

In the Vietnamese hospital it is still the custom for the family to camp near the patient's bed, sleeping under or beside it and cooking in the grounds. In some institutions they may supplement the regular hospital fare with the patient's favorite tidbits; in others they may be expected to provide for the patient's entire diet.

Traditional medicine (acupuncture, massage and herbal medicine) is practiced alongside modern medicine in the health service. It has its own medical schools and research institutes. In recent years more of the load has been put on the traditional branch because its methods are inexpensive and available. Although Vietnam has more physicians per capita than other countries at its economic level, the Western embargo and the shortage of money have often put modern methods and medicines out of reach.

VUI LÒNG
NGƯỜI MẸ MIỀN NAM

The Vietnamese health service has had its triumphs in spite of the enormity of the problems and the scantness of the resources. The bottom tier of the health system, the paramedic's station in every village, has brought basic health care and knowledge of hygiene and sanitation to the entire population. The DRV used this network of health stations in effective drives against malaria and other major diseases. Septic tanks helped to combat intestinal parasites by protecting the drinking water.

The end of the war in 1975 heaped major new problems on the health service. In some respects it lost ground gained earlier. For instance, campaigns to combat and prevent disease similar to those in the North had not been carried out in South Vietnam, so that many diseases remained endemic and had to be attacked anew. Malaria surged back. Mosquitos more resistant to DDT were finding millions of bomb and shell craters in which to breed. On the other hand, it dealt remarkably well with the 100,000 drug addicts and half a million prostitutes the war left behind in southern cities.

Western medical people give greater credence to acupuncture and herbal medicine than to some of the other traditional methods still practiced in Vietnam. One example is cupping, a practice obsolete in Western medicine for some time, in which the rim of a heated cupping glass is pressed on the skin. An example of the fruitful contacts that can be made between natural and Western medicine is the use of coconuts for intravenous infusions. The coconut is punctured in the same way as the bottle, clamped on the same stand, and the patient receives needed sterile fluid in a form his blood can accept, along with a bit of sugar and protein. The coconut keeps without refrigeration and any number can be obtained locally.

In the late Eighties health officials called attention to the seriousness of malnutrition, citing it as a factor in the high case rate of diseases, in shortened life expectancy, and in the continuing low productivity of the work force. This was a problem the health service could not solve, nor could it be laid to the past or the war. It came from the failure to get the economic engine started.

EDUCATION

The Confucianist social outlook is founded on respect for learning and the principle of advancement through learning. Education has been the key to upward social mobility in all ages and under all Vietnam's regimes. The traditional village schoolmaster taught the children the basic elements of Confucianist ethics and social ideology with some language instruction along the way. The high level of literacy achieved by this system declined rapidly during the French colonial period. *La mission civilatrice* did not include solid primary education for the natives. The French policies that created a class of landless wage-laborers in rural areas created a Vietnamese white-collar class in the cities, where even illiterate workers sent their children to elementary school. Secondary education was much less common, especially for girls.

But the French deserve credit for initiating the use of *quoc ngu* in teaching Vietnamese. The *lycées* they set up for their own children were attended by select members of the Vietnamese élite. Eventually a number of Vietnamese would be educated in France. Many would become supporters of the French against their own countrymen, but some would be instrumental in driving their patrons out of the country. Later on, socialist Vietnam would adopt the *lycée* as the model it looked to in its educational system.

The resolute and resourceful literacy campaign which the Viet Minh began during World War II proclaimed education was to be the individual's road to social advancement, just as it was the country's road to modernization. Even before the end of the First Indochina War poverty had ceased be a complete barrier to education in the DRV, where public school enrollment increased from 190,000 in 1945 to 4.7 million in 1970.

After 1975 a re-run of the literacy campaign was necessary in the rural areas of the South. At the same time the orthodox-minded leaders took steps to 'disinfect' the South's school system. They sent down schoolteachers from the North, and those in the South were required to 're-qualify' in special courses before resuming their teaching careers. The revolution's goal in the field of education was nine grades of universal compulsory education. In an otherwise conventionally structured system, adult education is available free to age forty-five in special schools, in the workplace, and by correspondence.

127. *Traveling through Vietnam is an adventure. If you car does does not break down, there are always natural obstacles. Here the fortunate owner of a luxurious means of transportation, a motorcycle (in working condition at that), is pushing his way down a flooded road.*

The need for reform of education was addressed in 1979. The Confucianist tilt toward literary subjects was replaced by a new triple literary-ethical-occupational emphasis so that the schools could supply workers, technicians, and managers to the economy. Another year was added to the secondary schools in the North. The reform also aimed at catching up with the outside world in science and technology. A Support Your Local School campaign was launched to elicit voluntary contributions from citizens.

By the mid-Eighties the commission for educational reform announced that the goals had not been met, but literacy was again on the rise: 2.5 million were entering the school system every year, and three million pre-schoolers were in day-care centers and kindergartens. The regular public schools had an enrollment of 12 million, nearly one-fifth of the entire population. The number of grades was increased from 10 to 12. Enrollment in specialized high schools and colleges stood at 300,000. Yet, even if the country could claim more than a million people with scientific and technical training, the quality of education was still low. Critics in the mid-Eighties found higher education to be too inflexible and stereotyped; technical education leaned toward nonrural occupations when modernization was needed most in agriculture. In the early Seventies only 10 percent of coop managers had completed the nine-grade school, and only one per cent of graduates from agricultural colleges were actually working in the cooperatives. There is not enough occupational diversity in the rural areas. Young people want to get out of farming, and farm managers think of those with education as 'overqualified', already out of place on the farm. The yearning for development is great. A great deal of energy to fuel that development is waiting to be tapped.

Meanwhile, absence and dropout rates were still high. In 1980, 85 percent of secondary students were dropping out before graduation. The choice they faced was this. If they specialized in an occupation, they committed themselves to close-ended careers, for only the academic curriculum led to higher education and the chance of entering the élite. Those who gambled by not learning a skill and later realized they would not go to college faced this fact by withdrawing.

Nor are the students the only ones demoralized with the school system. Underpaid teachers are unhappy, and even the most dedicated must become discouraged by having to train students for practical jobs when the schools lack the equipment for this.

The Soviet Union, which has shown a particular interest in education, has given the Vietnamese considerable help in tackling these problems. Between 1959 and 1980 its educational assistance program trained some 60,000 specialists and skilled workers and reached thousands of other vocational students in secondary school. Soviet universities and institutes represented the major avenue for Vietnamese graduate students to obtain advanced and specialized training.

128. *Channels of the Mekong River meander through cultivated fields in the delta — the country's greatest rice-growing region. It has a warm and humid tropical climate with an abundance of rain during the summer. ▷*

129

129. *Section of the delta growing rice, coconuts and papaya. Fishing nets are spread along the banks of the river, which has abundant fish and shellfish. The major problem of the delta area is the regulation of riverflow.*

130

130. *A canal in the delta dotted with vessels resembles a city street. The total absence of infrastructure makes it difficult to settle and develop this area, although it seems to be rich in petroleum and natural gas.*

131.   Busy traffic in the delta seems as disorganized as bicycle traffic on city streets. This leads to frequent minor accidents that invariably end with both parties shouting insults at each other.

132.   Luxuriant delta vegetation frames the river. Areas closest to the waterline are rich in mangrove trees, while coconut and date palms, mango, and pineapple grow in less waterlogged parts.

133.   The carrying pole is an ancient device which enables Vietnamese peasants to carry enormous loads. During the war heavy artillery and ammunition were transported in this way. ▷

134-136. A congregation of diverse Vietnamese craft. From the ferryboat (previous page) to the fisherman's coracle, everything that can float is used for transportation. The abundance of waterways and dearth of alternatives on dry land has given great scope for inventive creation of watercraft. The country is crisscrossed by about 25,500 miles of rivers and 2000 miles of canals.

137

A young peasant women heads for her boat after shopping in the market.

138.   The young crew of a pirogue on
the Mekong pose with pleasure for my
camera. Village children learn to row at
an early age and can often be seen alone
in their pirogues up the canals of the
delta.

138

139, 141. Heavy rains and overflowing rivers transform the few roads of the delta into streams. A country road flooded during the monsoon season proves that nothing can interrupt everyday activities.

140.   This overcrowded car making painful progress through the flooded streets stands a good chance of getting stuck. Car traffic in Vietnam is very sparse. Private ownership of cars was prohibited until a few years back, and they are still considered a status symbol and a luxury. The rare specimens in circulation usually serve as collective taxis.

141

142

142. *An old Montagnard in traditional dress in front of his house which has been built on stilts for protection. This village, Trang Phuch, only 5 kilometers from the Cambodian border, was armed and fortified by the Green Berets during the war.*

143. *Montagnard women washing clothes in the stream which runs by Trang Phuc. While the inhabitants of the Mekong Delta use the rivers for transportation, the Montagnards prefer to move themselves and their goods by elephants.*

144. *Tiger, folk print on rice paper, date unknown. This is a fairly old specimen, but the date is difficult to determine since the same designs are used over a lengthy period.* ▷

145. *'Picture of Foreign Lands', painting on a paper scroll (detail), 14th-15th century, Nam Giang.* ▷ ▷

143

146. River landing near My Tho, one of hundreds of small fishing and farming settlements between Ho Chi Minh City and the extreme south of the delta.

147. A fisherman's son sits in the bow, while his father maneuvers the pirogue.

148. Every delta community spreads its circular fishing nets. The only task of the local boys is to empty them and fold them up.

149. This peasant tending ducks tidied up his hair to look better for my picture. I was amazed at the skill with which he maneuvered both the pirogue and his flock: like a good sergeant with well-trained recruits. Perhaps he was that once. ▷

150. A peasant staggers under his load of baskets made of bamboo, a material abundant in Vietnam. Apart from recycled war materials, everyday life depends on what nature provides. ▷ ▷

148

The Spirit and the Word

RELIGIONS

Vietnam's three principal religions – Confucianism, Buddhism, and Taoism – developed centuries before the Christian era opened and came to Vietnam second-hand from China. They are distinct, and yet they do not exclude one another. Vietnamese so often make devotions to more than one of them that some observers lump the three together as the religion of the country. Christianity began to gain followers among the Vietnamese population through the efforts of Catholic missionaries in the sixteenth century. The success of Protestant missionaries has mainly been among the tribal upland peoples. Cao Dai and Hoa Hao are latterday religions, both native to Vietnam.

Confucianism is primarily a code of social ethics. In modern terms it might not be far-fetched to call it an ideology. It does not focus on a supreme being, and Confucius laid no claim to divine revelation. Instead, he laid down the pattern of behavior expected of the individual – be he peasant, mandarin or the emperor himself – for the higher good, which is the welfare of the society as a whole. It is a conformist social philosophy, and the lines of authority are clear-cut: the subject shall be loyal and obedient to his emperor, the wife to the husband, the children to the father, and younger to older brother. The bonds of friend to friend, while not hierarchical, are just as essential to the health of the social order. The Confucian social order is class-oriented. Punishment, for instance, is appropriate only for the uneducated masses, while the educated and therefore superior man is kept in line by the emperor's good example. The emperor rules by mandate of heaven, and that mandate may be withdrawn if the emperor fails to honor and protect his subjects as the head of the social family. Confucianism is based on the belief that men are by nature good. A very important corollary of that premise is that goodness is perfected by education, in particular the literary study of the classics.

Buddhism, which centers on the individual's search for enlightenment, came into Vietnamese life by three routes. First, by the same Chinese route as Confucianism: Vietnam became a province of China at just the time when Buddhism was sweeping China, and this Mahayana version of Buddhism swept through Vietnam in the first centuries of the Christian era. Over the centuries Vietnam also

151. The Vietnamese are watermen by tradition, on both river and sea. The waters off the east coast of South China and the Gulf of Thailand have an enormous variety of fish. ◁

152. A fisherman bailing out his craft while holding on to a navigation marker on one of the canals of Phan Thiet. The can fastened to the pole serves as a lamp that burns at night to prevent larger boats from running aground.

received infusions of Hinayana Buddhism, its other major branch. One source was the holy men who from time to time landed on the Vietnamese coast direct from India. Some of them were revered long after their brief stay. The other was through cultural interchange, including intermarriage, with the Cham and Khmer peoples in the south whom the Vietnamese displaced or overran in their expansion.

The two Buddhisms are like litmus indicators of the Chinese and Indian influence in Vietnam. Mahayana ('great career') came down from the north from China, and Hinayana ('small career') represents the extent of Indian influence. The 'career' refers to the individual's aim in the practice of his religion. Mahayana expanded existing 'small' careers by adding the career of the Boddhisattva, a being qualifying for nirvana and yet remaining behind to teach others the way. This religious world inhabited by a host of deities provided a doorway to Buddhism wide enough for newcomers to import their previous divinities, complete with superstition and magical notions far from pure Buddhist doctrine. This is one example of how Confucianism, Taoism and Buddhism became so interwoven in Vietnam in spite of their fundamental differences.

Mahayana Buddhism denied the Buddhist clergy the strong doctrinal foundation they used elsewhere in Indochina to set themselves apart. Buddhist monasteries were fewer and less powerful in Vietnam. With Confucianist elements so woven into the institutions of the state, the Buddhists were rarely able to play a strong political role, and they were the target of restrictive laws in times when the Confucianists were politically dominant.

Taoism (pronounced 'dowism') has two branches. Both originated in China and both spread into Vietnam. The philosophical Taoism credited to Lao Tsu (604 B.C.) glorifies the simple life. The way ('tao' means 'way') offered to the individual is to achieve contentment through harmony and tranquility, by bending with nature rather than wrestling with it. The philosophical Taoist can be content with a minimum of comfort, and he prizes culture above possessions.

Religious Taoism offered a quite different 'way', suggesting that sorcery, divination and magic could build inner strength, restore youth and bestow immortality on earth. This movement drew part of its philosophical foundation from the other Taoism. In the external aspects of religious practice it imitated Buddhism, and for a time enjoyed great favor in China, but Buddhism largely absorbed it. Taoist temples in Vietnam today are relics of an abiding popular receptiveness toward the occult, astrology, divination and sorcery. But the ideal of a tranquil round of life close to the soil in an autonomous village at peace with its neighbors, revered by the Taoists, also survives.

Catholicism is the only form of Christianity to have taken much hold in Vietnam. The Portugese planted the first missions in the late sixteenth century. The missionaries invented *quoc ngu*, the Roman-alphabet transcription of the Vietnamese language. For better than two hundred years it served only the Catholic Church and helped it to spread to all parts of the country.

The 1954 Geneva Accords gave Vietnamese 300 days to move north or south of the 17th parallel. The Catholic Church encouraged its flock to vote with its feet against the anti-religious regime in the North. The 600,000 Catholics who heeded that call, half of the total number in the North, were the largest group in the nearly 900,000 who moved South. In the mid-Eighties there were estimated to be three million Catholics in Vietnam, two million in the South and another million in the North.

Vietnamese were receptive to Catholicism from the outset. The French Jesuit Alexandre de Rhodes caused a stir in church circles with his astounding conversions. Catholic success might have been even greater if the Vatican had taken a more lenient stance toward polygyny and ancestor worship. During the French colonial period the Catholic Church was finally on a firm footing and free of the repeated persecutions which had plagued it.

Cao Dai and Hoa Hao both originated in the southwestern region of the country bordering Cambodia. Both are Buddhist in foundation, but Cao Dai is far more eclectic in drawing also on Taoism, Confucianism and Christianity. It stemmed from the revelations of Ngo Van Chieu in 1919, and grew under its first pope, elected in 1925. Moses, the French admiral Duclos, Joan of Arc, Sun Yat Sen, the sixteenth-century poet Nguyen Binh Khiem and Victor Hugo are some of the strange bedfellows in the Cao Dai panoply of saints. The Cao Dai Cathedral outside Tay Ninh is an impressive structure and the interior, with its central eye representing the supreme being, has a certain phantasmogoric beauty.

Hoa Hao is more a splinter group within Buddhism that developed in the late 1930s. Its distinctive doctrinal feature is that it takes Mahayana Buddhism a step further in a quasi-Protestant direction by teaching that the individual may worship God directly without the intermediary of an official church.

Both of these sects have been so deeply involved in politics as to have had their own armies. Both were encouraged by the Japanese in their effort to bolster anti-Western sentiment during the war. In 1945 they worked with the Viet Minh for a time, but soon set out on an anti-Communist course and collaborated with the French during the First Indochina War. In 1955 they supported the French puppet Bao Dai, and Diem had to overcome them to take power. After unification in 1975 they offered considerable resistance to the new government, and have since been natural targets of Communist suspicion. The regime dismantled the hierarchy of the Hoa Hao, and left room for worship only at the individual level.

THE LANGUAGE

The idea of Vietnam as a cultural crossroads, useful in examining its religious currents, is also helpful in looking at the

Vietnamese language. While Vietnamese is distinct and spoken by a compact group, its origins can be traced in separate directions. The idea that the Vietnamese people owe their origin to a blend of mountain dwellers and seagoing people is partly based on the different strains that can be detected in the Vietnamese language. Mon-Khmer, a major language group in the mainland Austroasiatic family, absorbed influences from sea-based Austronesian peoples. Tonality and a number of grammatical features came into the language with an infusion from the Thai group of languages, and last, in historical times, Chinese contributed a substantial vocabulary in many important areas such as government, literature, philosophy and technology.

When the Chinese absorbed Vietnam (Nam Viet) in 111 B.C., the Vietnamese had no written language. Those upper segments of Vietnamese society which became involved in the Chinese administration learned to speak and write Chinese. They had their own way of referring to the characters, which has given rise to the term Sino-Vietnamese, as though during the Chinese occupation there was a version of bastardized Chinese used by the Vietnamese or a version of Vietnamese made visible thanks to Chinese characters. That was to come later. During the thousand years of Chinese occupation the written language used was exclusively Chinese. In fact Chinese remained an important language for official and literary writing right up to the eighteenth century. In 1942-43, when Ho Chi Minh found himself in a Chinese prison, he took pains to write his poetry in Chinese so that his suspicious jailers could read it.

Vietnam achieved its independence in 939, but it was over three centuries later, in 1282, that the transcription of the vernacular was codified. The essence of *chu nom* was to form a new written language with Chinese characters by separating the sounds and the meaning they represented. Two centuries later the Emperor Le Thanh Tong would establish *chu nom* as a literary language by collecting and publishing the work of Nguyen Trai and by using this language in his own accomplished poetry. Nguyen Du's *Tale of Kieu*, the recognized masterpiece of Vietnamese literature published in 1820, was written in *chu nom*.

Christian missionaries have always been (and still are) major contributors to linguistic knowledge. They were the front-line messengers expected to convey The Word. To perform their mission effectively, they had to supply the Bible, the liturgy and their own sermons in a form accessible to their native congregations. The Catholic missionaries in Vietnam spoke Romance languages. It was natural for them to use Roman letters as a medium to represent the sounds they heard and the language they eventually would speak.

In 1651 Alexandre de Rhodes used this transcription, known as *quoc ngu*, in a dictionary and short grammar of the Vietnamese language he published in Rome. This book incorporated his own work and that of other priests who had tackled the problem before him. One powerful reason why they devised this system was that neither they nor their parishioners had the command of Chinese characters required to use *chu nom*.

For two centuries *quoc ngu* lived exclusively in the Catholic Church, rejected by the Vietnamese authorities along with everything else Christian. It gained currency when the French colonial authorities gave it their wholehearted support. Aside from its practical benefit, they were anxious to replace as many traditional institutions as they could. *Quoc ngu* became the official transcription of Vietnamese in 1906, and is now the universal written form of the language.

What seems so improbable is that a system devised for such a narrowly defined purpose should have done its job so well and gained acceptance so quickly. There is an important practical reason: the speed at which a schoolchild learns to read and write his own language. Chinese characters take years to learn, but a child can assimilate the *quoc ngu* representation in a matter of months.

In *quoc ngu* accent marks are added to Roman letters to represent on paper the pitch or tone that identifies the word the speaker intends. A few examples will illustrate how important the tone is in distinguishing meaning. These sequences of letters may have the following meanings depending on the tone and the corresponding accent marks.

ma: ghost, cheek, but, tomb, equine, rice sprout
toi: I, dark, mediocre, sin
hai: two, to pick (fruit), shoe, marine, to fear, harm
ba: three, hug, grandmother, poison, dregs, haphazardly

Quoc ngu did not replace *chu nom* until the twentieth century. The Viet Minh were first to exploit its full potential. Even before 1945 they began a determined and effective drive in the areas they controlled for every person over age eight to acquire basic reading and writings skills. Students were called upon to teach their elders. By 1950 they had created the country's first universal general education system using the Vietnamese language and *quoc ngu*. In 1975 they tackled the problem of the estimated 1,400,000 illiterates of working age in the southern population. A new drive aimed at them claimed 94 percent success by 1978.

PROSE LITERATURE AND THEATER

Over the last one hundred years Vietnamese writers have explored all the major prose genres familiar in the West, including journalism, short stories and the novel. And some early prose has been preserved: national legends, literary renderings of folk tales, Buddhist tracts, lives of eminent figures, imperial messages to commanders in the field and public documents dating back to the fourteenth century. But drama and poetry have the deepest roots in Vietnamese literature and are the most distinctively Vietnamese.

Vietnam has four kinds of theater. The two Western-related

forms are Cai Luong ('revived theater'), an operatic form which developed from choral and orchestral concerts in the early decades of this century, and the thoroughly Western 'spoken theater'. The two traditional genres are the highly formalized Tuong, and the Cheo, which includes much improvisation.

Tuong theater is said to derive from the performances represented on the ancient bronze drums uncovered by archeologists in northern Vietnam. At some later point it was influenced by the classical Chinese theater, which celebrates real historical events in Confucian terms to inspire loyalty to one's country, devotion to one's emperor, and reverence for one's father.

The Tuong combines declaimed speech, dance, mime, acrobatics and fencing with music from gongs, tambourines, and native string instruments. A succession of tableaus calls up events from the hero's life. The music creates the atmosphere: imminent threat, defeat, or nocturnal calm. The actors accomplish changes of time and place with conventional gestures. For instance, an actor can indicate the passage of several years by walking from one side of the stage to the other, or a change of place by circling his position three times. There is no scenery, and the props are simple; the actor needs only to carry a riding crop to have a steed beneath him or an oar to walk the deck of a ship. Makeup, however, is elaborate and explicit.

The canonical formalism of the Tuong can be suggested by the way a character enters the action. He approaches the stage with head bowed, his face hidden. Once in place, he straightens his robes and strikes his pose before lifting his face to the light. At the gong signaling the audience's permission he introduces himself and explains his character's part in the action.

The Cheo is a folk product that developed in the age of Vietnam's independence. This is theater performed without props in the village common house. It is so popular among the peasants that two northern delta provinces have between them about 1000 amateur and semiprofessional companies. They offer the audience a plot which must be resolved happily. Justice is always done, crime never pays, virtue never goes unrewarded. The gaiety and humor central to every play imparts a holiday atmosphere to a Cheo performance. Cheo plays re-enact on the stage the action of verse novels. Their language is simple and clear and combines the acutely visual metaphors of Oriental poetry with folksy adages. The dances reflect motions occurring in daily work in the field.

POETRY

Great kings often reveal their greatness by finding great advisers. So it was with Le Loi (who reigned as Le Thai To) and Nguyen Trai. Together they rebuilt the national culture following the devastation methodically worked on it during the twenty-year Ming occupation from 1407 to 1428. During Le Loi's brief reign Trai served him as counselor and ambassador, corresponded with the Chinese general on the emperor's behalf, tutored the emperor's son who would reign as Le Thai Tong, wrote the country's first geography, and established *chu nom* by publishing a collection of verse in this transcription of the vernacular. When Le Loi died, the poet withdrew from public affairs to a life of reflective idleness in his native Kon Son. In his poetry he often contrasted this idyll with the petty intrigues of court life. Later, however, his former pupil persuaded him to head the committee conducting the civil service examinations.

In 1442, when those exams had just been completed, he retired to Kon Son. One day the emperor stopped by on his way to military exercises in the neighborhood. At his next stopping place the emperor suddenly took ill and died. The courtiers accused the poet's wife, who was in the emperor's entourage. Hearing this, Trai immediately set off to rescue her from this intrigue, but was himself caught up in it. He and his family were all executed to the third generation by direct and lateral descent. Nothing by halves. His memory was rehabilitated by the great Le Thanh Tong (reigned 1460-1497), a poet himself, who ordered the collection and preservation of his poetry and other writings.

Nguyen Binh Khiem (1491-1587) was the principal poet of the sixteenth century. Like many other literati, he established his social position through the examinations and had a brilliant career in public service under the Mac family. Like Nguyen Trai, he retired from court life to his country residence, which he called 'White Clouds', a name he also used as a pseudonym.

The poetess Ho Xuan Huong was the major figure in the poetry of the Tay Son era at the end of the eighteenth century. She is one of those writers about whom we know nothing and everything. Her biography is almost a blank page, but the poetry reveals a rare and bold sensibility.

Nguyen Du's *The Tale of Kieu*, published in 1820, is the centerpiece of Vietnamese poetry and the most popular literary work in Vietnam. Its accessibility is evident when even illiterate people can recite whole chunks of it. Technically, it is a *truyen*, or long verse narrative, written in *luc bat*. This six-eight couplet can stand alone like a *haiku* to capture a single image in its 14 syllables, or it can sustain a lengthy narrative without becoming monotonous. Nguyen Du (1765-1820) did not invent the story of Kieu but lifted it complete with customs and setting from a sixteenth-century Chinese novel. Its dramatic extremes and the rattling pace of its plot might make it a successful opera. The opening pages introduce the young woman Kieu and her family. She exchanges vows of undying love with the young scholar Kim and delivers a wise and tender speech on why they should be chaste until they marry. This idyllic situation is shattered when Kim is called away to arrange the funeral of an uncle in a distant city, and Kieu's home is invaded by constables. She sells herself into marriage as the only expedient to save her family. Alas, the man who buys her has been sent on a collecting trip to procure virgins for a bawdy house. This 'husband', as mean a villain as ever drew fictional breath, cheats even the madam by deflowering Kieu before delivery.

Just as with opera, the plot is not the point, but the songs and who sings them. This is where Nguyen Du excels. No reader can fail to love and admire Kieu. Beautiful, resourceful and accomplished, she can knock off a bit of extemporaneous verse whenever the situation requires. The little poem that follows is not from *The Tale of Kieu*, but the reader will see that Nguyen Du knew an image when he saw one and could make others see it.

> *the moon looks down a well*
> *and sees itself reflected*
> *in the bottom, smooth as glass*
> *until a hand draws water.*
> *the bucket ripples the image,*
> *which shakes and then returns.*
> *my heart is the well*
> *in which I see myself.*

THE PRESS, RADIO AND TELEVISION

In the late 1980s Vietnam had 350 periodicals of various kinds. The national and provincial newspapers adhere strictly to their respective lines of reportorial territory. The more numerous ethnic minorities have newspapers published in their own languages. Some popular magazines aim at the general audience and others address women, young people or other particular groups in the population. There are also journals, news bulletins and newsletters for more professional and specialized audiences.

The electronic media were represented by over fifty AM and several FM radio stations, and by a central television network broadcasting from Hanoi and several regional stations.

In Vietnam the mass media exist to serve party policy. No bones are made about that. They are monitored not only by the culture ministry, but also by the propaganda and training depart-ment of the party's central committee. While their principal aim is to support and promote party policy and to 'edit' the information available to the public, they do make an effort to educate the population. Letters to the Editor columns may be manipulated and confined to 'healthy and constructive' criticism, but they do furnish the public a small channel to voice annoyance. In mid-1987 there were signs of a groundswell of *glasnost* forming in the journalistic profession. The Soviet Union has built two ground stations to receive Soviet television broadcasting via satellite. In January 1990 Turner Broadcasting System won a tough battle against the U.S. trade embargo and obtained permission from the Bush Ad-ministration for a similar station to bring its 24-hour CNN news channel to Vietnamese viewers.

153.   The City Hall of Ho Chi Minh City, today a bright yellow color. When the city's name was still Saigon, its façade was greyish, or perhaps a dirty white. On April 30, 1975, around midday, the yellow flag of the South, with its red stripes, was lowered for the last time, and the keys of the town hall were handed over to the victors.

154. *Before 1975, this central square and the well-known Tu Do Street nearby were crowded with bars and nightclubs overflowing with beer and dollars. Today the area is still busy on a Saturday night, but all the attractive places of entertainment have been closed down.*

155. *Street in the Cholon quarter of Ho Chi Minh City, once inhabited entirely by the rich Chinese merchant class, which even today, though on a much smaller scale, runs the best supplied market in all Vietnam. To anyone who remembers this quarter from prewar times, it resembles a ghost. Many of the 'boat people' were Chinese from Cholon.*

154

155

156.   A monument erected in honor of Tran Nguyen, one of the legendary Tonkinese army commanders, in the central market square of Ho Chi Minh City.

157.   Traffic on a large boulevard in former Saigon. In the past, cars and motorcycles prevailed, then only bicycles were left. Now, finally, motor vehicles are being cautiously re-introduced. The city spreads over 500 square miles and includes 18 urban and suburban districts.

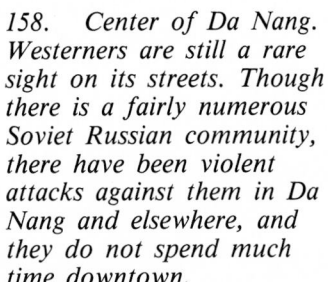

158. Center of Da Nang. Westerners are still a rare sight on its streets. Though there is a fairly numerous Soviet Russian community, there have been violent attacks against them in Da Nang and elsewhere, and they do not spend much time downtown.

159

159. An arcade in Hoi Han, one of the most beautiful small places in Vietnam, with all the fascination of small colonial towns in Asia. Its house façades, stained by tropical damp, are painted green, yellow, and red.

160. The Catholic cathedral in Ho Chi Minh City, with a statue of the Madonna in the center of the square. Built during French rule, it has remained the stronghold of the Catholic Church and Vietnam's estimated 2.5 million Catholics, mainly concentrated in the South. The Communist government has never banned or openly persecuted any religion, but in the last 15 years the Catholic Church has been subject to serious restrictions affecting both the clergy and the faithful.

161

161. 'The Festive Return of the
Military Man', painting on a paper
scroll (detail), 14th-15th century,
Nam Giang.

162

162. Arhat (Buddhist saint),
painting on a wooden panel (detail),
16th-18th century.

230

163. *'Picture of Education',
painting on a paper scroll (detail),
14th-15th century, Nam Giang.*

163

164. *'The Festive Return of the
Civil Servant', painting on a paper
scroll (detail), 14th-15th century,
Nam Giang.*

164

166. Detail of the central decoration of the temple of Phay Giao, between Ho Chi Minh City and Xuan Loc, with the Buddhist symbol of the swastika. 166

167. The small Buddhist temple to Phay Giao, one of the most beautiful in the country in spite of its recent date. It was completed in 1967, when the economy of the South still permitted investment in projects not directly related to bare survival. 167

165. A Montagnard cemetery in Trang Phuc. These people are mostly animists, practicing religions quite distinct from those of the Vietnamese. Note the imitation elephant tusks to the right of the tomb. The grave, I was told, belonged to a village headman who had owned many elephants.

168

168. The Confucian temple in the middle of Ho Chi Minh City incongruously serves traders as a place to display bathroom fittings. Most Vietnamese of Chinese descent practice Confucianism. From 1975, the government began persecuting the ethnic Chinese, many of whom were forced to flee the country.

169. *Polychrome lacquered wood sculpture of the meditating Buddha, 18th century (?).*

170. *One of the elephants adorning the Imperial Palace Park in Hué.*

171. *Elephant-shaped pot for warming an alcoholic drink, Hanoi, 16th-17th century.*

172. Hué's Imperial Palace in the center of the Citadel still shows signs of past splendor, as well as traces of war. This city of 200,000 inhabitants occupies a very romantic setting. The river flowing through it is called River of Perfumes (Song Huong), for its waters are said to reach the city covered with flower petals which fall into it on its way down from the Truong Son Mountains.

171

172

235

173.	This small temple stands on an isle in the middle of a lake called 'The Returned Sword'. One of Hanoi's favorite recreation spots, it derives its name from a legend.

174.	The railroad bridge on the Red River in Hanoi, destroyed many times in U.S. air attacks. Today the reconstructed bridge has two bicycle lanes apart from the railroad tracks.

174

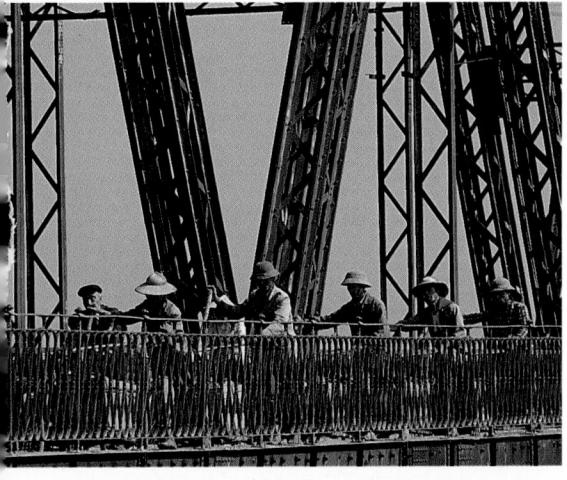

175. View of Hanoi's West Lake, formed from a bend of the Red River. According to a legend, this is where a vicious fox with nine tails lies hidden under a huge rock.

175

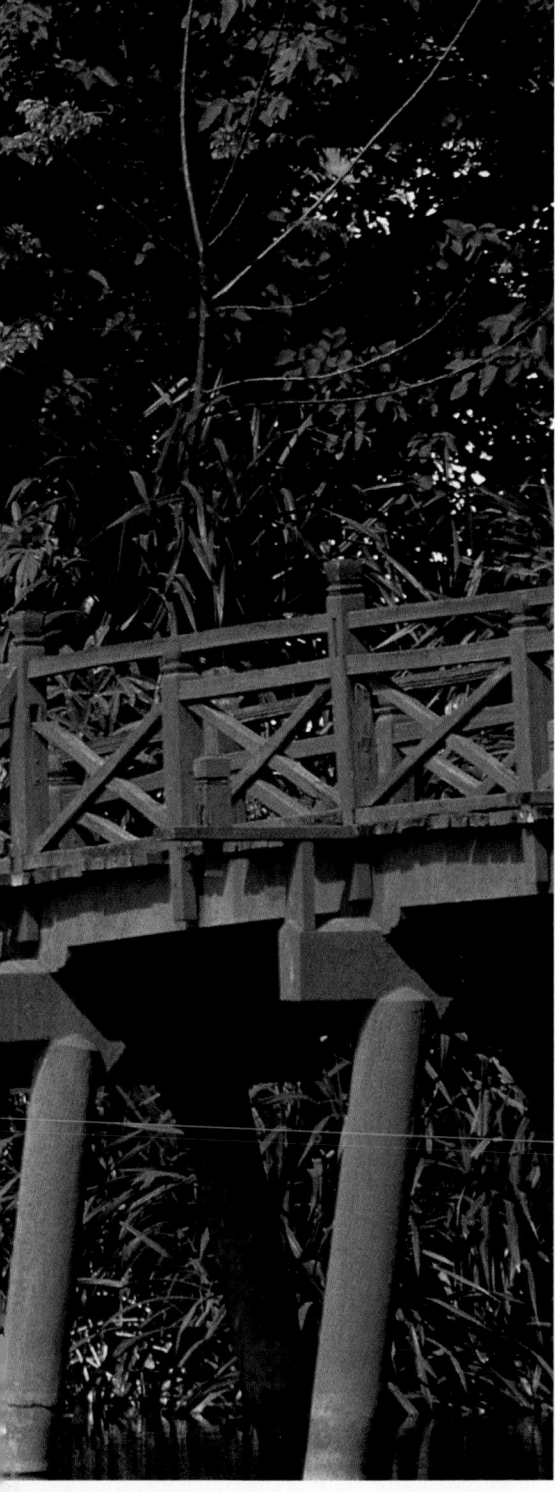

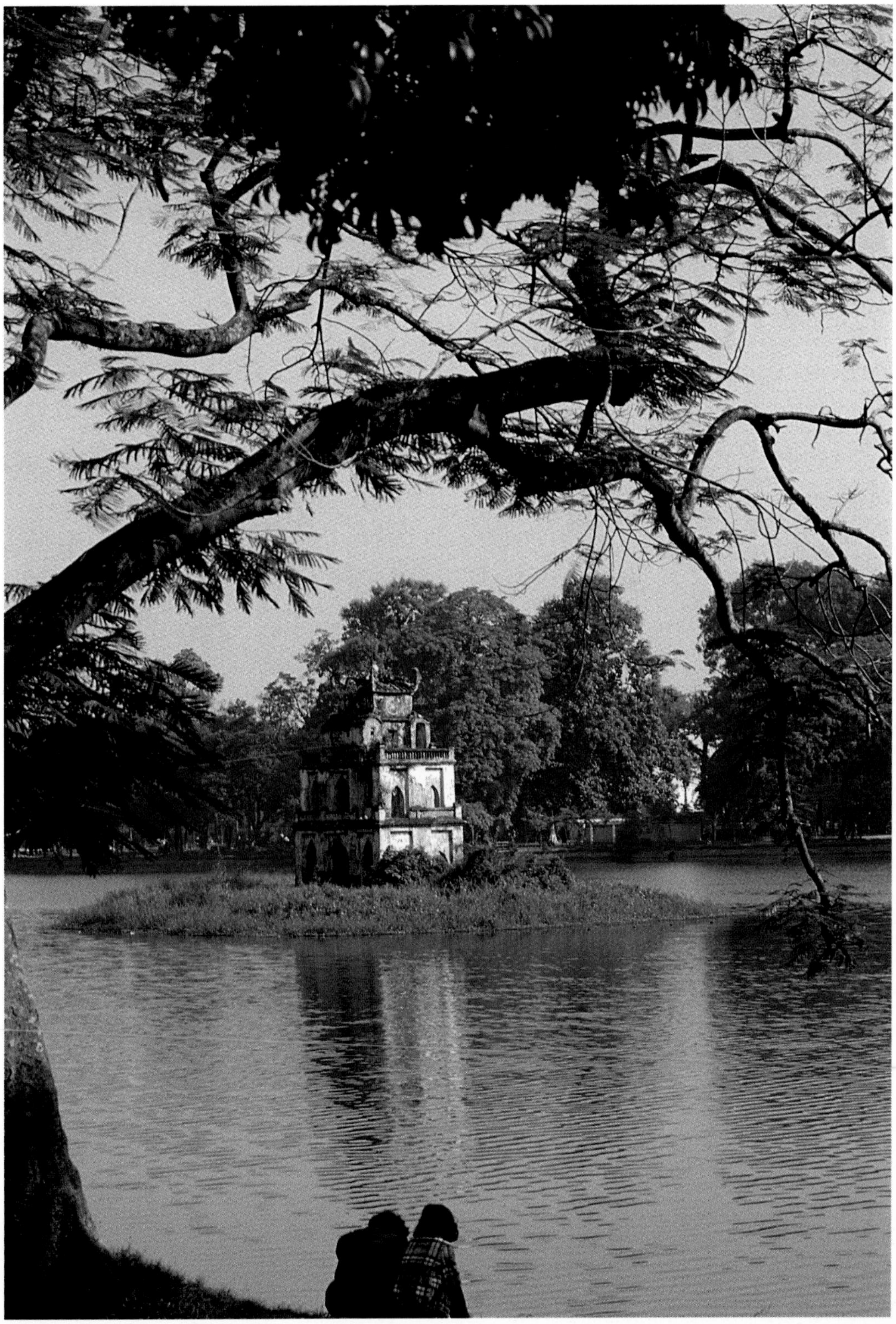

176.   A Hanoi policeman on his motorcycle with antiquated sidecar, on the square near Lake Hoan Kiem. This city of 3 million inhabitants, built on an arm of the Red River, has 4 central quarters and 12 peripheral districts. The central axis runs along the tracks of the old streetcar leading from Silk Street to Dong Xuan market.

177.   While vehicles wait in an endless line for the ferry, dozens of itinerant vendors appear, offering their wares. The price for foreigners is always much higher than for local folk, often a tenfold markup.

177

178

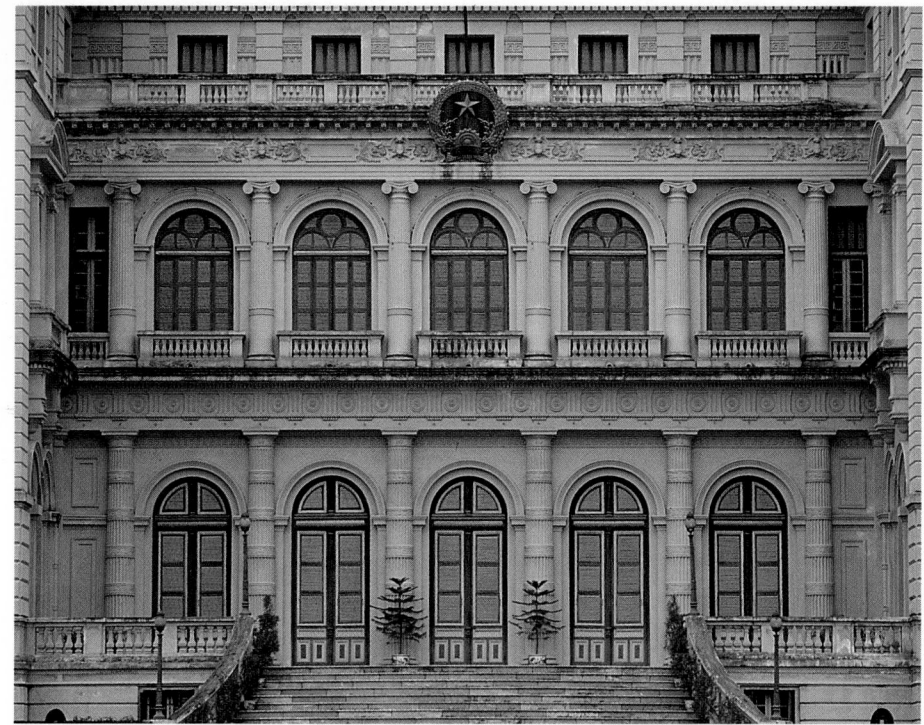

178. The Presidential Palace in Hanoi, built during French rule. The city owes its most attractive neighborhoods to the French.

179. A sugar-cane seller negotiates with drivers while they wait for the ferry to arrive.

179

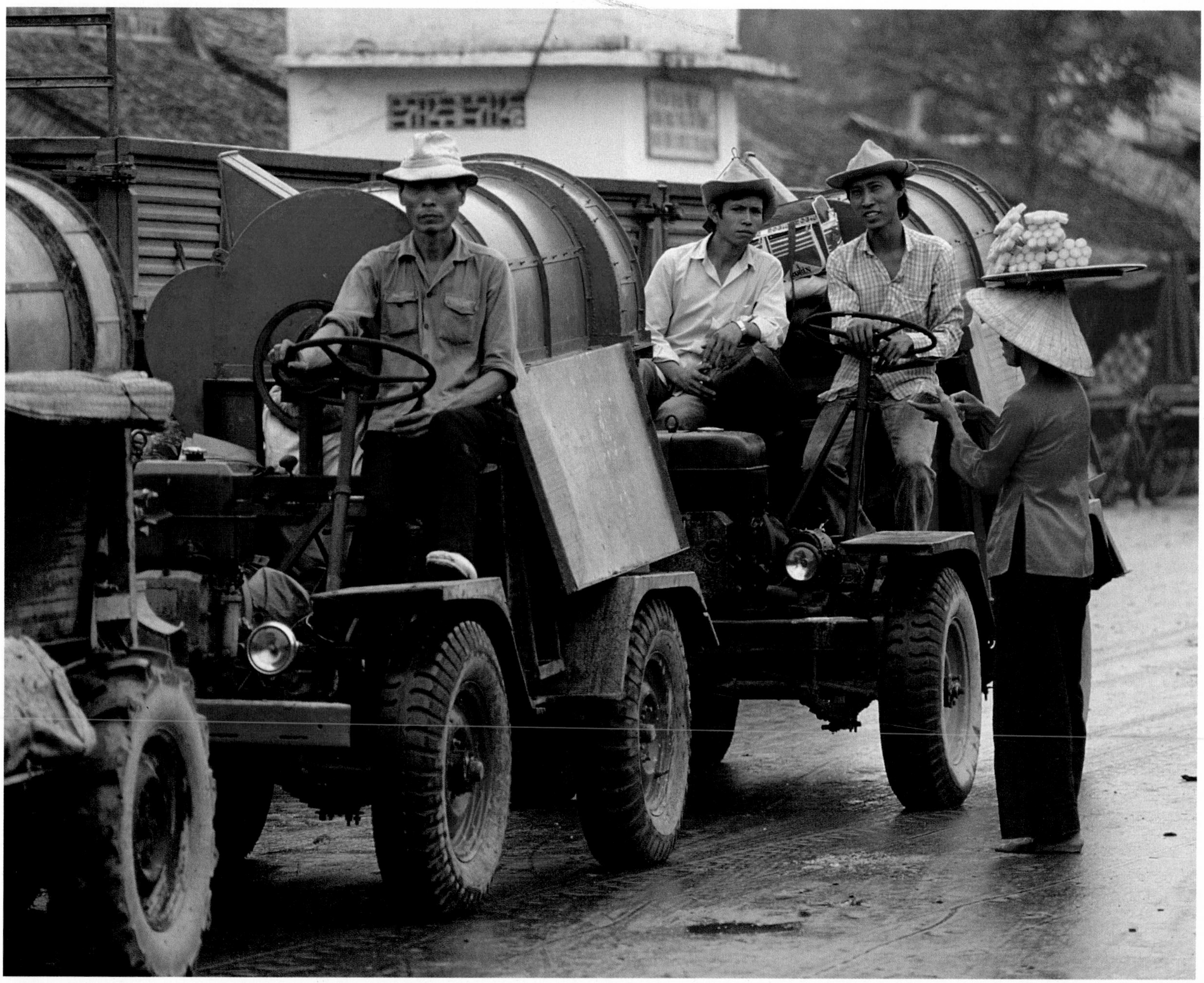

Major Cities

HANOI

In the year 1010, the story goes, the founder of the Ly dynasty set out to find a site for the capital of his new empire. At the banks of the Red River a dragon in flight above him lighted half the sky with its radiance. The emperor heeded this omen and named his new capital Thang Long ('ascending dragon'). Today this is the name of one of Hanoi's central hotels and its newest bridge.

The city prospered at the meeting of rivers and streams extending eastward throughout the delta to the coast and northward and westward into the uplands of Vietnam and southwest China. Nestled in an elbow of the river, it has lived a thousand years below levees that keep out the Red River at high stage. In the 1979 Census Vietnam's capital city had a population of 2,570,905.

There are two spans over the Red River from the city proper. The Long Bien Bridge was formerly the Paul Doumer Rail and Highway Bridge. When France adopted Hanoi as the capital of its lands in Indochina, Doumer initiated the highways and railroads leading out of the city. They fanned out eastward to Haiphong, south to Saigon, northwest to tap the tin ores of China's Yunnan Province, and more directly north into the heart of China. The Thang Long is a mile-long double-decker rail and highway bridge built six miles north of the city center with Soviet help.

Hanoi has two airports. The older Gia Lam is nearby, across the Red River, while Noi Bia is a good hour's drive north of the city. The national air line provides service to Hué, Nha Trang (south-central coast, near Cam Ranh Bay), Danang, the upland cities of Pleiku, Da Lat and Buon Me Thuot, and Ho Chi Minh City. There are also direct international flights to Bangkok, Moscow, Prague, Berlin and Khabarovsk.

The pervasive rumble of congregated automobiles, taken for granted in any modern city, is missing from Hanoi's sound pattern, leaving only the lightweight buzz of motorbikes, intermittent motorcycle growl, and the metallic thudding, screeching and clanging of passing streetcars.

Hanoi has frequent power cuts and shortages of drinking water. One trouble is that flood control often restricts use of the available water power. But the immense Da River project will by itself increase Vietnam's power supply threefold when completed in the Nineties.

180. *Statue of Confucius in a temple in Ho Chi Minh City.*

This is a great city to tour by bike. The quiet of Hanoi's streets is a precious virtue. If only it did not mean poverty and underdevelopment. The French residential architecture is still stately and solid, and one sure sign of prosperity, when it does come, will be the restored freshness of its façades and shutters. The city has abundant parks, lakes and streams. The most famous and central is the Lake of the Restored Sword, which the French called Petit Lac. The story that goes with this lake is that in olden times when the country was languishing under the Ming (early fifteenth century) a fisherman named Le Than brought up in his net a blade with the inscription 'Do as Heaven bids!' Le Loi, the general, saw this blade, and later, when he was in the jungle leading the rebellion against the Chinese, a glimmer in a tree that caught his eye turned out to be a sword. It goes without saying that he used that sword with merciless skill against his enemies and drove the Chinese from the country. Later, as he was rowing on the lake, the Golden Turtle appeared and said, 'Lord, the time has come to return the sword to the Dragon Emperor'. Le Loi returned the sword, and the lake was given its new name. The turtle may be the most authentic feature of the story. Large turtles can be seen basking on the edges of the island that supports the Turtle Tower.

West Lake, which the Red River is said to have hollowed out in one of its rages, figures in one of the versions of the death of the fabled Trung sisters. The Chinese records say that Ma Yuan captured them and sent their heads to the emperor. Other versions simply say that they died in battle. But the cult which has revered their memory to this day has them drowning themselves here in Hanoi's West Lake.

The National Museum of Vietnam is on the south bank of the river. Its collection of Southeast Asian bronzes is said to be the world's finest. The museum was previously named for Louis Finot, who headed the French research into Southeast Asian history and philology initiated in the 1890s. Even those most critical of France's performance as a colonial power acknowledge the important interest it showed in the past of Southeast Asia, the solid scholarship it initiated, and the high standards it set in this field. Northern Vietnam is today thickly dotted with archeological sites and ongoing explorations. Four ancient capitals are within easy reach: Co Loa, the late Bronze Age capital, is a dozen miles to the north. Me Linh, seat of the Lac lords and home of the Trung sisters, is located 40 miles to the northwest. Luy Lau, the Chinese provincial capital whose citadel was besieged by the Trung sisters, is located east of Hanoi. Hoa Lu, some 40 miles to the southwest, is the capital founded by Dinh Bo Linh in the tenth century, when the country was called Dai Co Viet.

In November the rainy season, which turns the plains into a vast lake of mud, relents as winter approaches with the crachin. Men and women don old woolen sweaters or padded jackets over their shirts and blouses, and children are given caps with ear flaps.

There are several ancient monuments, including the pagoda of the Great Buddha, so named because of its 12-foot-high bronze statue, and the One-Column Pagoda, which dates from the eleventh century. The Temple of Literature (Van Mieu), also built in the eleventh century, was dedicated to Confucius and was the basis of Vietnam's first university.

Signs in Russian are not the only evidence of Soviet-Vietnamese friendship in Hanoi: book stalls have a wide selection of titles in this language. Translation from Russian has also been a thriving industry over the past twenty-five years. Soviet films are often shown in the movie theaters, and Vietnamese television relies on Soviet sources for much of its material.

HO CHI MINH CITY

Ho Chi Minh City (a.k.a. Saigon) looks more European than Oriental, more French than Vietnamese, more provincial than metropolitan. One reason the French look is so strong is that the fighting of the French and Spanish to defend their new prize in 1859 nearly demolished it. Later the French rebuilt to their own taste. Magnificent trees arch over the avenues as in French provincial towns. In the aftermath of a nationalist and Communist revolution it has been seen as a source of 'Western decadence', a charge perhaps hard to deny when one recalls the size of the military establishment centered here only two decades ago.

Ho Chi Minh City is situated far enough (42 miles) from the coast to be sheltered from the typhoons off the South China Sea, which occur regularly on the coast during the rainy season. The rain during the southwest monsoon is not steady, but intermittent, occurring usually at night or late afternoon, and is seldom heavy. Ho Chi Minh City's temperatures moderate during the dry season, ranging from the 50s in the early morning hours to the 80s at midday.

The Saigon River is the main waterway and a feature that shapes the city. In 1974 the city's commercial port could berth 30' deep-draft vessels at one time, it had moorings for transshipment to lighters in the middle of the Saigon River, and its New Port had four deepwater berths and several small ones. Eight major highways lead from Ho Chi Minh to other parts of the country. Ho Chi Minh City has international air services to Bangkok, Moscow, Khaba-rovsk, Prague and Manila. Domestic lines go to Hanoi, Rach Gia (on the Gulf of Thailand), the islands of Phu Quoc (Gulf of Thailand off Kampot, Cambodia) and Con Son (Poulo Condore, the penal island due south in the South China Sea).

Ho Chi Minh City has a high concentration of consumer goods industries for both domestic and foreign markets. In the Eighties these accounted for 30 percent of the country's industrial output and grew at rates of over 26 percent in 1980-1981 and 1983-1984. The place to go shopping in Ho Chi Minh City is Ban Thanh Market. In 1983, when the reform initiated in 1979 was losing steam, its cloth merchants and restaurants were taxed so highly for their space that many had to close. The more liberal policies of the late Eighties are bringing it back to life.

Ho Chi Minh City's street names are like a checklist of Vietnamese history. They commemorate the country's heroes, poets, emperors, warlords and other outstanding figures: Nguyen Hué, the ablest of the Tay Son Brothers; Le Loi, the fifteenth-century liberator; Nguyen Du, author of *The Tale of Kieu*; Hung Vuong, who founded the Hung dynasty...

Saigon's population has grown rapidly and accelerated in this century, doubling from a quarter of a million in 1907 to nearly half a million in 1943. In the mid-Fifties refugees flooded in from the North. Later, when the fighting resumed in the South, the warfare in the countryside drove more and more southerners to seek refuge in Saigon. The massive inflow of dollars created a huge service sector to employ some of the newcomers. But when that large, but temporary, bulge of the city's economy shrank to nothing in the mid-Seventies, Saigon became a city groaning under a burden of overpopulation. The 1979 Census counted 3,420,000, and that was after the drastic postwar efforts to relieve the bloating by moving people to the New Economic Zones.

HUÉ

Hué is a small place located where Vietnam's waist is pinched to its slenderest. When Gia Long chose it for Vietnam's capital in 1802, he was moved by more than loyalty to Nguyen tradition. Its central location appealed to the man who took his imperial name from the principal cities of the north and south. Perhaps he was interested in the site's geomantic advantages – the shelter offered against evil spirits by the pine-covered hills on three sides, one of them called the King's Screen. Those hills might also have a military appeal to a veteran of decades of defensive warfare. And although Hué is only eight miles from the sea, it sits astride the Perfumed River, a stream knee-deep in the dry season and waist-deep in the wet season, so that only light and shallow craft can navigate it. On at least one occasion, the French fleet, which took full advantage of Vietnam's long coast, turned further south because it could not make its way to the capital.

In any case defensiveness and conservatism in outlook and government were the mark of the Nguyen emperors in the nineteenth century, and ironically had much to do with the country's vulnerability to French invasion. Gia Long's ambitious architectural projects in Hué follow a pattern similar to the Confucianist bent of his public policies. What could be more defensive than a walled palace within a walled compound within a high-walled citadel? He imitated Beijing's Forbidden City in the massive bricked-over earthworks that enclosed the pavilions and courtyards of the imperial palace and the residences of the royal ministers and officials. The tower known as the King's Cavalier guards the main gate to this ensemble. In colonial times the business district and houses of French officials were outside the walls, and so was the real power.

The stone buildings show the effects of sitting under the wet side of the mountains. Hué is one of the most rain-soaked spots in the country. This region gets as much as 120 inches of rainfall. The summer and fall are wet, the winter dry. Monthly average temperatures range from 85° F (29.4° C) in July down to 69° F (20.3° C) in January.

In the present scheme of things Hué commands a much reduced domain as the seat of Binh Tri Thien Province, whose population is about two million. Riverboat lines, the coastal highway and the north-south highway link it to Danang, the central region's port and commercial center, located 60 miles to the south.

Hué's setting is bucolic. Surrounded by paddies, canals and streams, it is not a big industrial town, but these days leans toward tourism. Its handicraft industry working with glass and ivory (one answer to the question of what happened to the rhinos and elephants) has a long tradition.

The tombs of the Nguyen dynasty are located in the hills outside the city. Geomantic principles may have had something to do with this perfect marriage between setting and the works of man, but the parks and gardens are one of the few examples of Vietnam's long tradition in the art of landscaping. The large urns are for burning incense.

In the nineteenth century the emperor would perform the Nam Giao rites every three years on a sacred hill outside the city. To perform this ceremony on behalf of the entire nation, he and his ministers would purify themselves three days in advance. Then amidst clanging bells and booming drums they would roast a young buffalo and perform the rite of burying its blood and hair. As awesome shadows darted from the torchlight, they would offer jade, silk, rice, meat and flowers before the altars of Earth, Heaven and the imperial ancestors.

DANANG

The French name for this picturesque harbor was Tourane. It was the port at which the earliest Europeans called most frequently in their rivalry to establish factories and trade. Its natural harbor at the mouth of the Han River has close protection on the north from an island and a mountain spur that dips into the sea. A similar peninsular feature on the south side is connected to the mainland by a low isthmus. The possibilities for impregnable defense were obvious. A good place, thought some, to lure Chinese junks from China's southern provinces if they could be provided with a steady supply of opium to take back with them. The island of Callao, which can be seen off the coast to the south, appealed even more to the French and British for its harbor and its potential as a stronghold.

Danang is the capital of Quang Nam-Da Nang Province, which had over 1.5 million people in 1979, when the city itself had a population of 320,000. Although its harbor does not have the depth for large vessels, it is the most important seaport in central Vietnam. The north-south railway built under the French reached it in 1930. It is also on the coastal highway from north to south and has scheduled domestic air service.

Danang stands at the heart of what was the kingdom of Champa. The visitor can evoke the glories of that highly artistic culture by viewing the Cham towers and remains of Cham cities in the vicinity. An extraordinary collection of relics from nearby archeological explorations is displayed in the Cham Museum.

It was here that the United States began its huge buildup of ground troops in Vietnam when in March 1965 it landed 3500 U.S. Marines to provide protection to the U.S. airfield located outside the city. In March 1975 the fall of Danang and Hué, following defeat of the South Vietnamese forces in the highlands, were important signals to the leadership in Hanoi that an all-out strike at Saigon could be successful.

A 1978 treaty accorded the Soviet Union access to the naval and air facilities at Danang, giving it a logistic link for naval operations and support point for intelligence gathering. Missile systems are thought to be installed. The Soviet aircraft stationed at Danang include large antisubmarine planes. Thus Danang is one of the cities where the Soviet presence is quite evident. Its beaches, among them the famous China Beach, make it one of the favorite stops on the Soviet tourist's itinerary. The Soviet consulate in Danang has on at least one occasion been the scene of violence evoked by resentment of this latest of 'foreign intruders'. In 1990 the Soviets were recalling elements of their air force from this base as part of their general retrenchment.

Danang is noted for its marble, which was used in the Ho Chi Minh Mausoleum in Hanoi.

The area's textile industry draws upon the silk and cotton grown in the region. Hui Anh, 30 miles to the south, is a center for silk spinning and weaving. This town of some 60,000 was one of those subjected to the brutal authority wielded by the South Korean Marines stationed there from 1965 to 1973.

DALAT

Dalat is a French mountain town some 50 miles from the South China Sea. The setting of small lakes rimmed by pine groves is alpine, and the early twentieth-century architecture echoes Savoie, Alsace, Normandy, the Basque country and even Belgium. But at an elevation of 5000 feet there is mimosa, bougainvillea, poinsettia and a thousand varieties of orchid.

It is no accident that the word 'alpine' occurs in most descriptions of Dalat, which is perched on a southern plateau in the Central Highlands. It was after all a Swiss – the remarkable Dr. Alexandre Yersin – who picked the site for a health resort.

Founding a city was all in a day's work for this extraordinary physician. Dr. Yersin worked with Roux on the diphtheria bacillus at the Pasteur Institute in Paris, introduced rubber and quinine to Indochina, discovered the plague bacillus in Hong Kong and developed a serum against it, founded a branch of the Pasteur Institute in Canton, China, set up a similar institution at Nah Trang, whose director he became in 1895, and helped to establish in Hanoi Vietnam's first medical school. He was eighty years old when he died at Nah Trang in 1943.

Some of the many lakes in the vicinity of Dalat are storage reservoirs of hydroelectric projects. Dalat's virtues are alpine, yet the five peaks that command the northern skyline are volcanic (inactive). On a clear day the coastline is visible from a nearby vantage point. Dalat has long had air, rail and road connections to Vietnam's principal cities, but in recent years all have experienced maintenance difficulties. The trip by road to Ho Chi Minh City, about 200 miles, passes through some of the country's most spectacular scenery, including half a dozen waterfalls near the route during the first 45 miles. It also passes through Bao Loc, home of the famous tea they serve in Dalat.

Dalat is the capital of Lam Dong Province, whose main economic pursuits are tourism, the growing of rubber, tea and coffee, flowers, fruit (especially strawberries) and vegetables, the mining of bauxite, and a cottage industry producing many interesting handicrafts. Woven baskets, crossbows, fabrics, dolls, and musical instruments made by the indigenous tribespeople are sold on the upper level of the market.

During the colonial period it served as a hill station for those with the time and money to escape the baking summer heat of Saigon. Its world-renowned hunting and the quiet of a pastoral mountain town were a change of pace for the Saigon upper class, which went to Vung Tau (formerly Cap St. Jacques) for its seashore holidays. Many of the city's élite families, French and Vietnamese, had vacation houses in both places. Dalat owes its eclectic architectural flavor, which enhances the alpine impression, to the French, who built villas in the town's prosperous early years.

HAIPHONG

Haiphong (1979 population 1,279,067) is the smallest of Vietnam's three autonomous municipalities, but one of its two busiest seaports. It is located 16 miles from the Tonkin Gulf on the Cua Cam River, and 63 miles southeast of Hanoi. A canal separates the northern business section from the quieter southern parts of the city. The town itself has few historic monuments to beguile the

181. A lonely helicopter circles the sky over the ruins of Quang Tri in 1973. After the Paris Treaty, under which the Americans withdrew, the burden of the war fell entirely on the South Vietnamese.

182. 1968: the U.S. air cavalry in full action. My first entry into the combat zone; only five days before I had been in Milan. ▷

183. With an American infantry patrol on one of their numerous 'search and destroy' missions. We are in the delta, and our assignment is to discover and eliminate all the Viet Cong. ▷ ▷

184. The 'Meade River' battle, northwest of Da Nang, is over. An NVA (North Vietnamese regular), in the center of the picture, has just left his hiding place and fired a couple of shots at a Marine (second from the left). He was captured and flown to Da Nang in our helicopter. ▷ ▷ ▷

visitor, but there are pagodas and archeological sites in the vicinity. The island of Cat Ba, beautiful and interesting in its own right, is an hour's ferry ride away; from there one takes a boat to tour Ha Long Bay.

The city's industries include cement, tin smelting, and chemicals, glassmaking, rice milling, meatpacking and soapmaking. There are small rubber, textile and leather firms, shipyards and docks. Zinc has been mined within the city limits. The Hong Gay and other coal mines are a few miles up the north coast. Hong Gay is said to be the world's largest open-pit anthracite mine.

Haiphong has always been instrumental and incidental in everyone's plans. It served the French as railhead and outlet for the raw materials they exported to France. They transformed it from a fortunately situated village into a large seaport and commercial and industrial center. During World War II the Japanese used it to extract rice, coal, rubber and various minerals to support their military campaign in Southeast Asia.

In late 1946, fourteen months after the DRV was proclaimed, the French were ready to press their claim in the North and began their campaign by attempting to restore their duty-collecting authority in Haiphong against popular resistance. A French gunboat opened fire on a congregation of people on the quay, initiating a week in which the French took the city with bombing and shelling. Some 6,000 people were killed, many of them members of the city's sizable Chinese community. The Viet Minh retaliated one month later with a major assault against French garrisons and civilians that marked the start of the First Indochina War.

During the Sixties and early Seventies it was known to newspaper readers worldwide as the seaport vital to the North Vietnamese war effort in the South. Its importance in this respect increased even more in the late Sixties when the Chinese were discovered 'interfering' with Soviet rail shipments across China (inspection, picture-taking and even substitution). During the war it could berth six vessels at a time, while dozens more could be unloaded by lighter in the roads.

The United States, which had bombed Haiphong's harbor facilities when the Japanese held them, maintained pressure on Haiphong with bombing by B-52s and carrier-based aircraft during the Second Indochina War. Operation Linebacker II, a campaign conducted in the last ten days of 1972, was the most severe blow dealt Haiphong, and is credited with bringing the Vietnamese back to the peace talks in Paris, where an agreement was signed the following April.

The Soviet Union has contributed substantially to enlargement and improvement of Haiphong's port facilties since the Fifties. The city has also figured prominently in the Soviet effort to build up the Vietnamese fishing industry. Haiphong is the home port for the Ha Long Fishing Cooperative, which operates 11 Soviet-built trawlers and annually supplies 5000 tons of fish and seafood for fast-freezing at the Haiphong Fish Processing Plant, also Soviet-built.

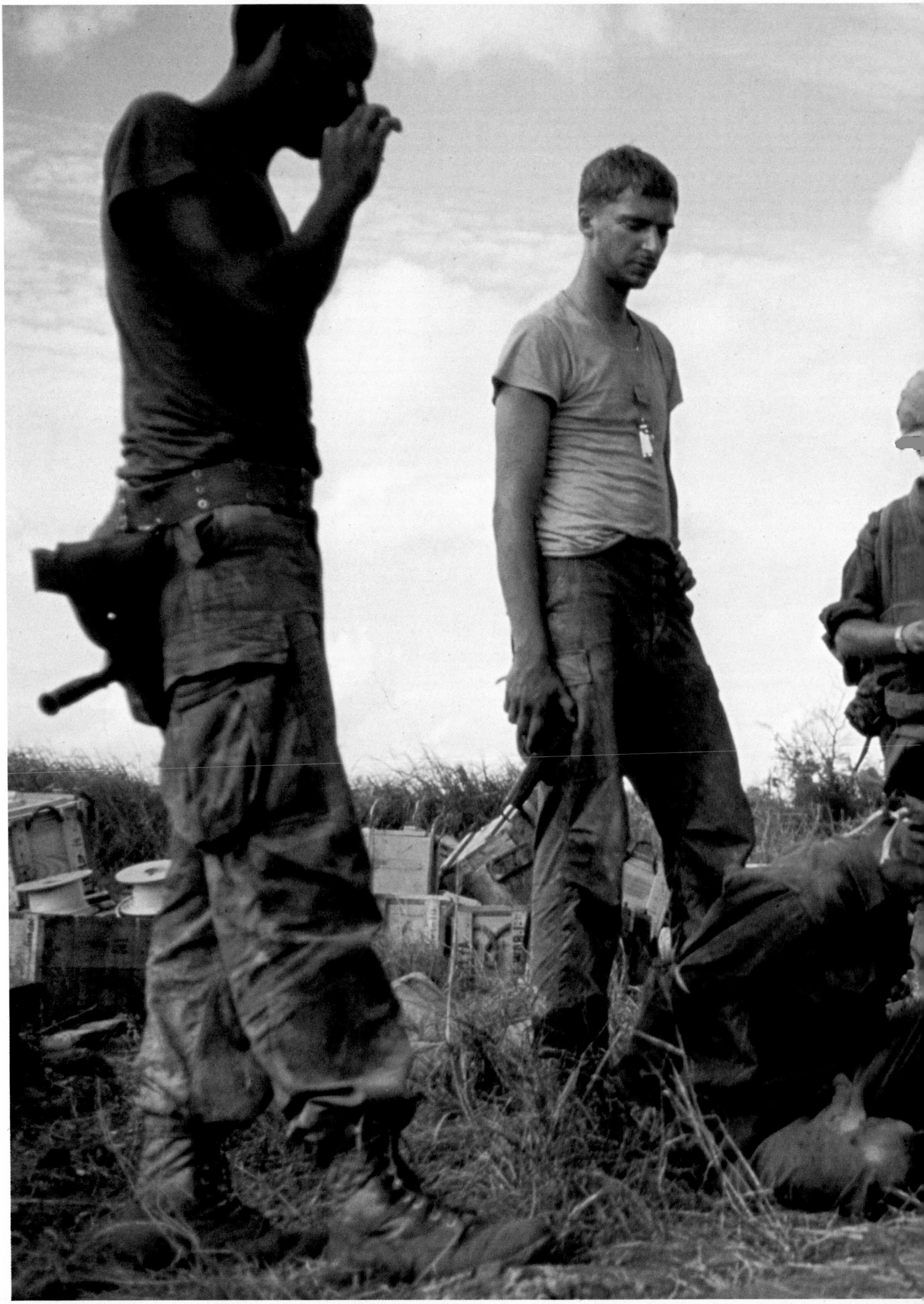

185.   Our patrol has been given orders to bomb a Viet Cong stronghold in a village. This is the result seen from ground level.

186

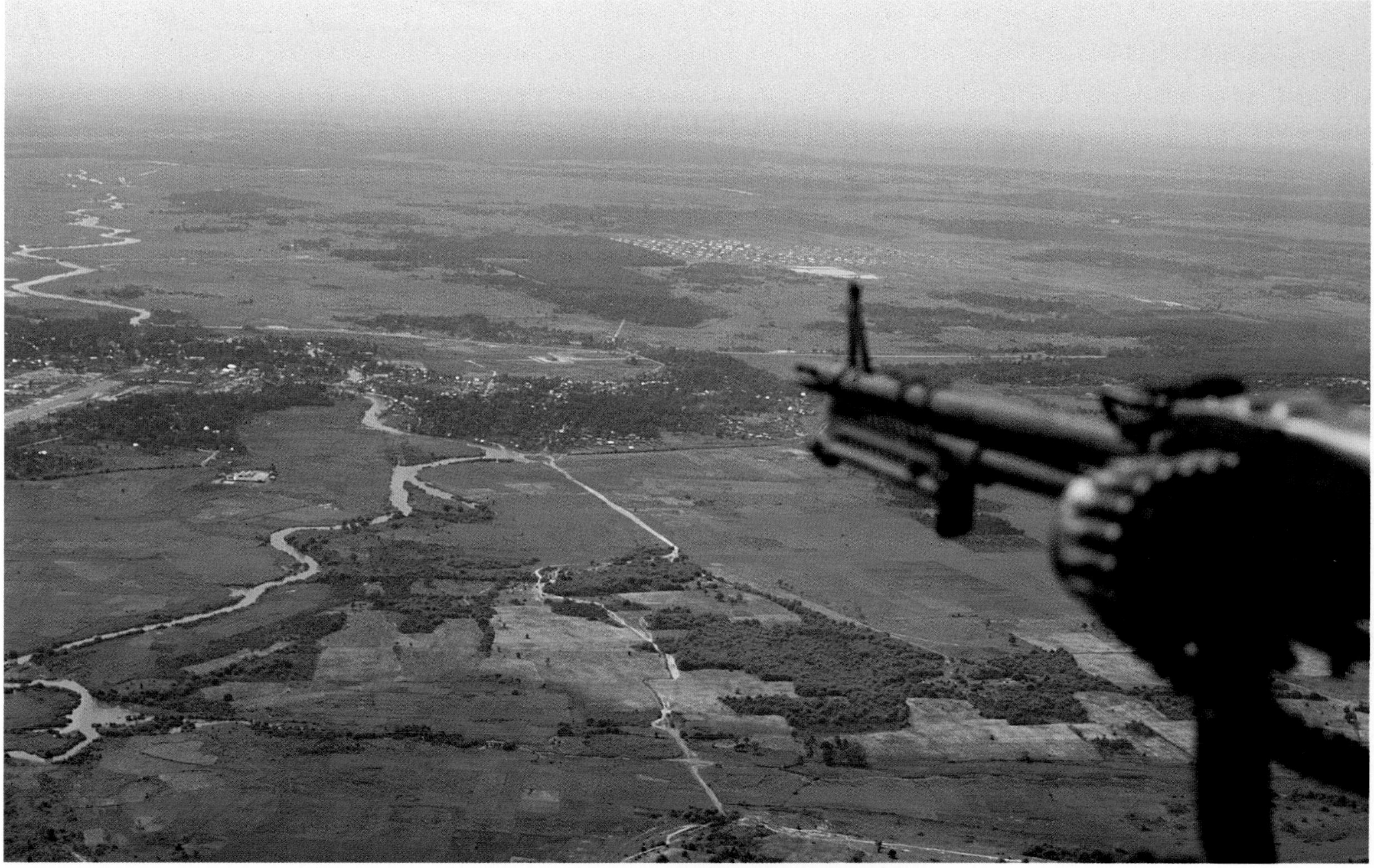

186. The delta area seen from a combat helicopter. Looking down, I often can detect no signs that a war is going on.

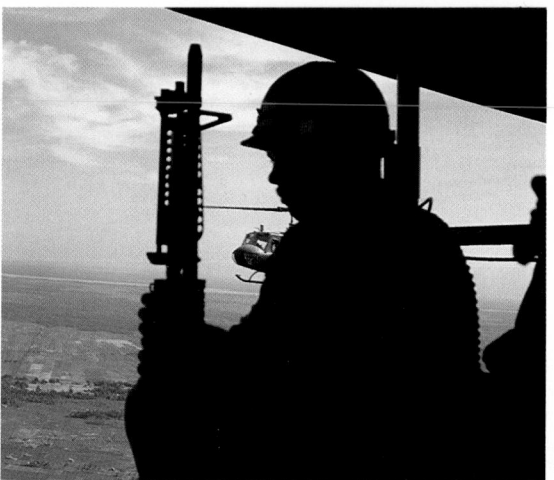

187. Flight with the air cavalry. While I get my camera ready, the men around me grow quiet and somber. Their good mood disappears with the takeoff.

187

189. Napalm and bombs attached under the right wing of an A-37 on a bombing mission in the delta.

188. Phantom taking off from the air base at Da Nang. In 1968 it was the busiest airport in the world, with the largest number of takeoffs and landings.

190. The jungle (what is left of it) after a battle. This hill in the Thai Nin zone is named 'Black Lady Mountain' (or Mountain of the Black Virgin).

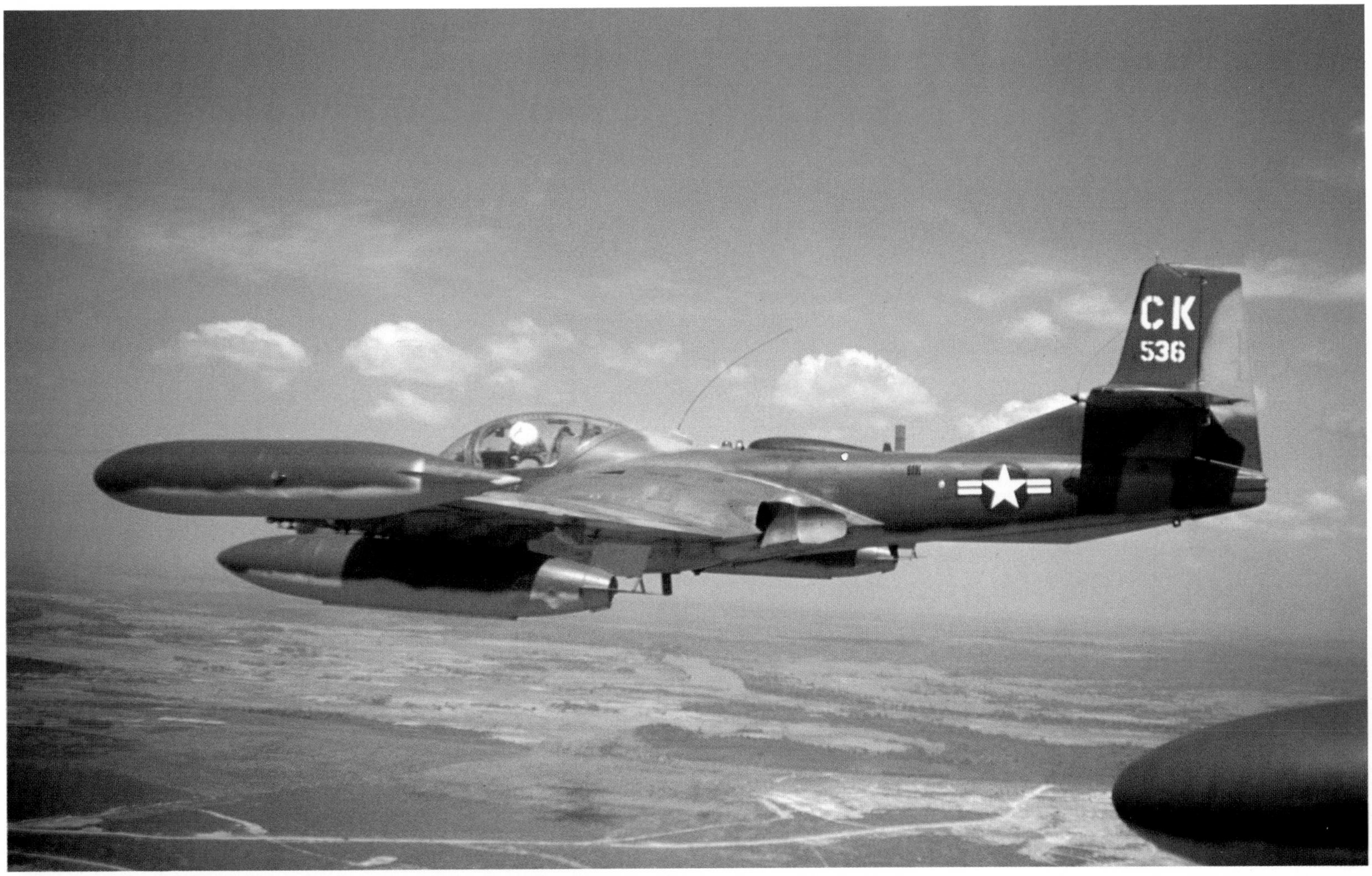

191

192

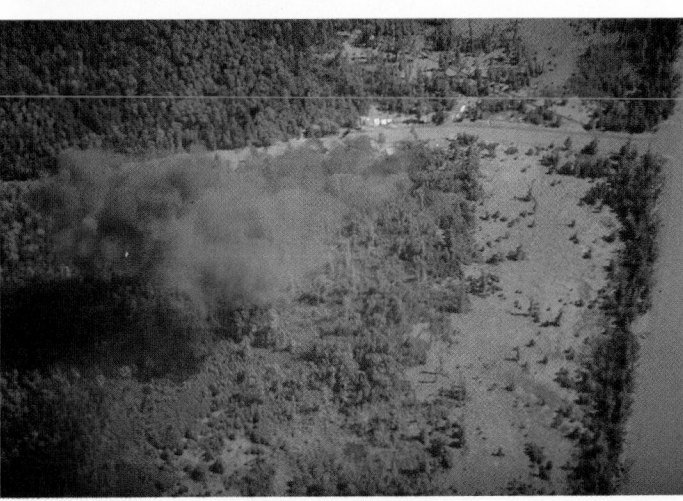

191. Our Cessna A-37 on a mission. We dive from time to time to release bombs and napalm. As we repeat the maneuver, my fear gives way to terror!

192. One of three pictures I managed to take on our bombing flights. It is difficult to control a camera at moments like these.

193

193. Marine guarding a small bridge near Da Nang. His orders are to shoot at everything he sees floating on the river, for it may prove to be a camoflaged enemy saboteur.

194. Orderlies carry a casualty in a 'body bag'. I took one picture and felt like a vulture. Even with dozens of soldiers around, not a sound could be heard. I was soon to find myself in a similar situation, but that time I could not bring myself to raise my camera.

194

195. *South Vietnamese Marine post on the south bank of the Thach Han River in Quang Tri. In 1973, this was the borderline between North and South. Across the river, military camps and flags of the North Vietnamese are clearly visible.*

196

196.   Fire base of the South Vietnamese Army with 105-mm cannon which could fire 8 rounds a minute and use various kinds of missiles. They were easy to dismantle and transport. These bases were meant to give artillery support to infantry troops within a range of 6 miles. All hell would break loose whenever precise coordinates of enemy positions were radioed in.

197.   Heaps of empty artillery shells under palm trees along the coast near Quang Tri. They give a general idea of how many shots were fired in combat. Like all military debris, even the shells have been recycled by Vietnamese civilians for everyday use.

198. South Vietnamese post among the ruins of Quang Tri, a fairly large city before the war, but razed to the ground because of the proximity of the DMZ (Demilitarized Zone). Twenty years later I returned to the very spot where I took this picture, but could no longer recognize it. In its place were only cultivated fields.

199. The small jeep in which my colleague, Ennio Jacobucci, and I traveled throughout South Vietnam, from Saigon to Quang Tri, in 1973.

200. A helicopter lands on Black Lady Mountain. During the war, the chopper was the only safe way of getting there.

201. South Vietnamese troops attached to a U.S. division on a 'search and destroy' mission looking for concealed weapons in villages.

201

202. The only way to attract a helicopter's attention is to fire a colored smoke signal. This helps pilots to estimate wind speed and direction on the ground, and to locate the landing zone in the vast green jungle. It is a moment of high risk for those on the ground, since they are directly exposed to enemy fire. ▷

203. Marines escort a blindfolded and bound North Vietnamese to the command tent. The Americans immediately handed over captured combatants to the South Vietnamese as prisoners of war, and took no interest in their future tragic fate. ▷

204. The highest peak of Black Lady Mountain near Thai Nin. It was an important strategic post and observation point for scanning the surrounding plains. In this zone, the Viet Cong dug dozens of miles of subterranean tunnels, with space for hospitals and military quarters, underneath U.S. installations. ▷ ▷

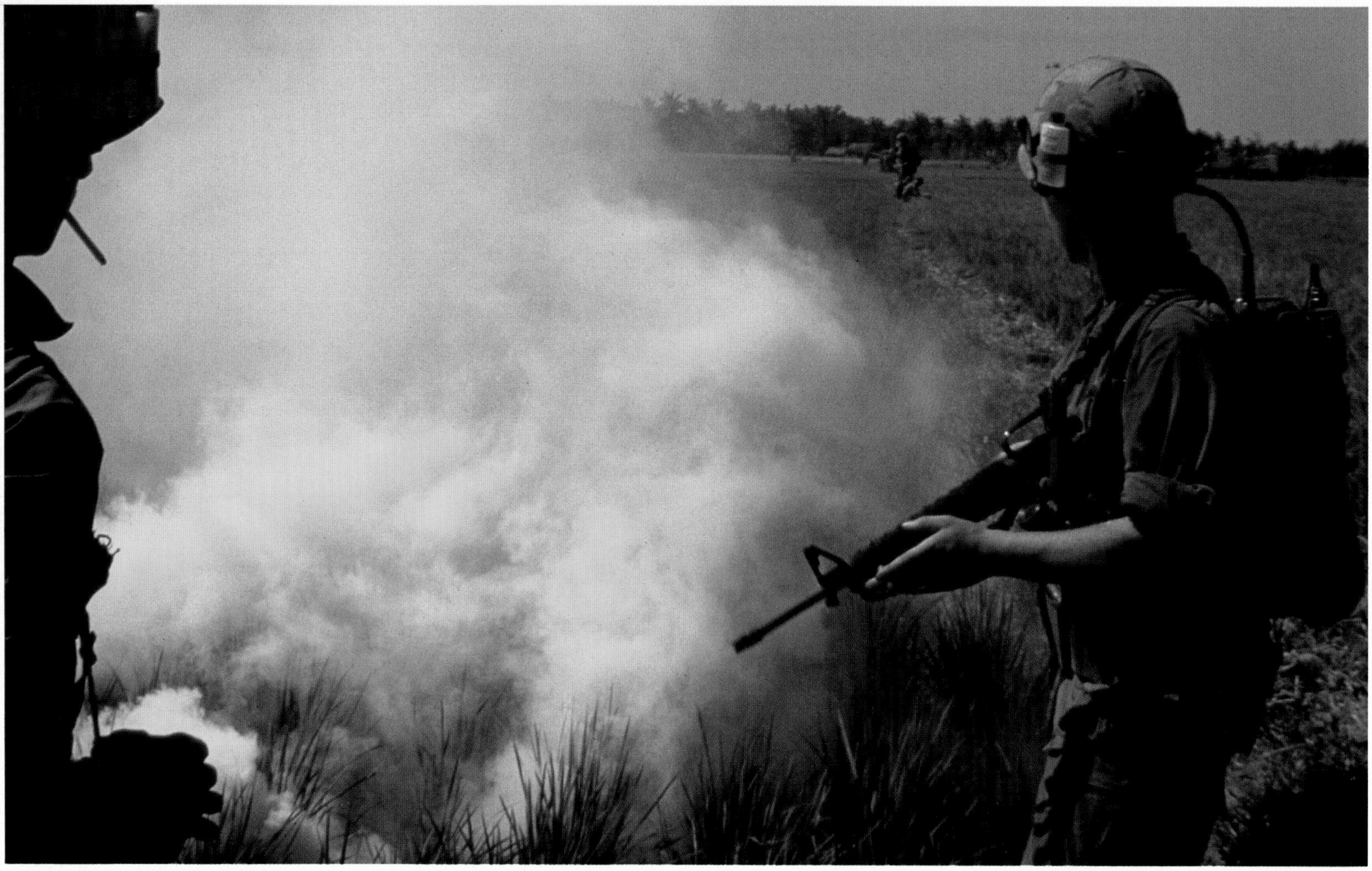
202

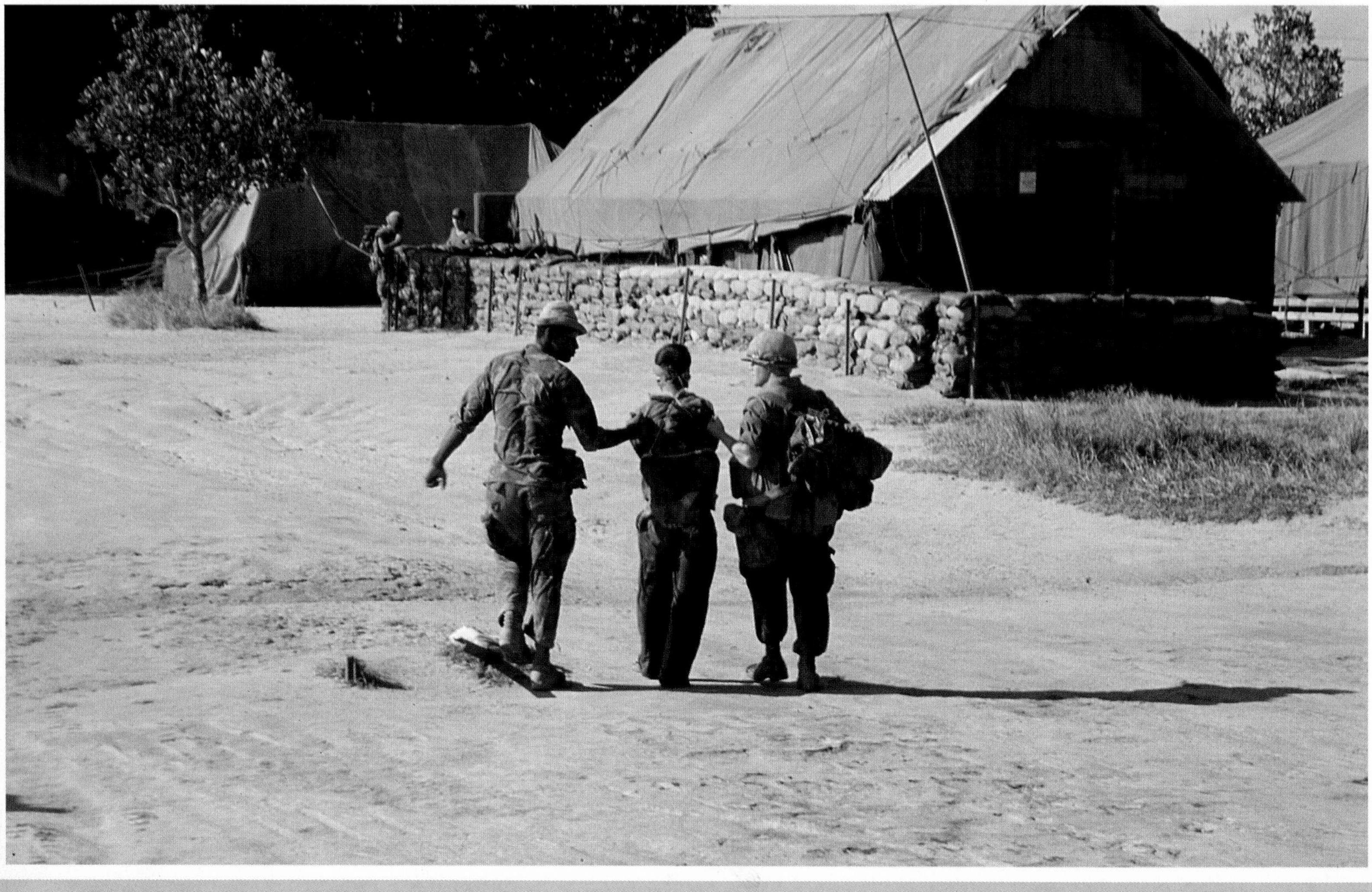
203

205

205. Ruins of Quang Tri after the battle to recapture the city. South Vietnamese flags flutter over the rubble. The stench of corpses lingered in the air months after the battle.

206. A CIDG (Civilian Irregular Defense Group): mercenaries originating mainly from non-Viet mountain tribes who provided flanking support for the Greek Berets. They were known to hate the North and South Vietnamese equally. How many of them perished has never been established.

206

208. *A soldier rests with an M-16 between his knees on a December day in 1968. After walking 20 hours through rice fields, we are not ready to face attack. I fell asleep, too exhausted even to eat.*

207. *U.S. soldiers who fought in Vietnam spent days on end soaked to the skin in the rice fields. Often the only dry things they had were attached to their helmets by rubber bands (90 percent of the time - cigarettes).*

210. Our doctor attempted to communicate with the woman through interpreters (on the right), who actually spoke very little English. After a few minutes of fruitless dialogue, the woman left in utter resignation with the child in her arms. The unmoved Tiger Scouts demanded cigarettes in payment for interpreting.

210

209. This woman arrived at dawn one morning in a small village near Mi Tho occupied by U.S. troops. Pressing her dead child to her breast, she was vainly seeking help.

211. Maimed children beg for alms in Tu Do Street in Saigon. They allow themselves to be photographed if paid, which I gladly do, hoping that my money will help. Incidentally, not a single magazine was interested in this picture.

211

212

212, 213. A small boy tending ducks drinks rainwater from a discarded helmet and keeps warm by wrapping himself in an army blanket, acquired who knows how. This style of dress seems normal to a 7-year-old born and raised in wartime.

214. *A peasant woman weeps as soldiers of my division arrest her relative suspected of being a Viet Cong because a concealed weapon was found in his house. The man was handed over to the South Vietnamese, and we never found out what happened to him.*

216.   *Green Beret captain in charge of the fortified village of Trang Phuc, on a high plateau near the border with Cambodia, attends rites conducted by the Meo (Hmong) tribe to appease their gods. The Meo are one of about 50 ethnic minorities living in the mountains of Vietnam. At the end of the ceremony, magic amulets were handed around, to be worn on the right wrist. I am still wearing mine.*

215.   *South Vietnamese soldier silhouetted against the sky at dusk. He was walking in a single file of soldiers along the road when I passed in my jeep. I yielded to the temptation to take this picture, although it may be a little theatrical.*

217.   *South Vietnamese checkpoint in an armored vehicle abandoned by the roadside between Saigon and Nha Trang. Perhaps it was not very comfortable to sleep in, but it provided solid protection against automatic gunfire.*

218

218.	The main street in Bien Hoa, the only road which connected the large U.S. air base and the capital, Saigon. The façades of the surrounding buildings show that it was the scene of some heavy fighting.

219.	Saigon street in 1968. Coils of barbed wire and sandbags form an integral part of the urban scene in the vicinity of public buildings and government offices.

220.	The City Hall, one of the most prominent buildings in Saigon, built by the French on the city's main square. A survivor of various regimes and wars, it still stands today, and now houses the City People's Committee.

219

221. *The Catholic church in Quang Tri soon after the South Vietnamese fought to regain control over the city in 1972. Twenty years later (as can be seen in pictures 56-58) its appearance had not significantly changed, apart from the removal of debris and artillery shells. The walls are still pocked with holes made by the thousands of bullets fired in street battles.*

222. *Detail of the church in Quang Tri.*

223. *Remains of a railroad bridge near Quang Tri destroyed in the war. It has now been rebuilt and restored to its former state.*

222

223

224. *South Vietnamese troops guarding
the railroad a few miles from Da Nang.*

224

Village Life

THE MONTAGNARDS

For two thousand years of Vietnamese history the uplands belonged entirely to the indigenous tribes. The upland cultures were generally impervious both to the Vietnamese culture of the deltas and to the Chinese and Indian influences that meshed or collided in Vietnam's lowlands. Over the centuries the upland and lowland groups did not establish fruitful or even amicable intercourse. At best the lowlanders ignored the hill people, who liked nothing better than to be left alone. In a harsher light the Viets harbored a bias against the mountain people; they feared the uplands because of malaria and dysentery, and it offered them few conditions for their kind of farming and their type of village. The Montagnards for their part harbored an enmity developed over centuries of bad experiences. At various times they have been pressured to adopt another way of life, their ancestral lands have been taken away and sold, merchants have cheated them, and they have been mistreated by military expeditions.

There are over 50 tribal peoples ranging in size from just over 100 members to over a million. They have in common their low-level subsistence economy, their preliterate or semiliterate culture, their animistic religion, and their lack of a higher social or political loyalty. On all these counts they differ sharply from the Viet majority in the lowlands. The also differ widely from one another in language, building styles, clothing and personal ornaments, the shape of the farming implements they make and use, their religious practices, and social relations in the village. They use a dozen distinct languages belonging to three major linguistic families, and 11 have their own writing systems.

In origin, some are descendants of ancient migrants from southern China who settled in the northern border regions, others are probably related to lowland natives of Malay stock who were forced into the highlands by successive invasions of Mongoloid people from China. Similarly, the Cham in central Vietnam are remnants of the kingdom that ruled the central coast until overrun by the Vietnamese in the fifteenth century, and the Khmer, forebears of the present-day Cambodians, ruled the Mekong delta region until displaced by the Vietnamese in the late eighteenth century. The Khmer and Cham are thus lowlanders. They and the

225. The great white Buddha I photographed north of Da Nang in 1973. It was encircled with barbed wire and seemed immune to bullets. In a country scarred by gunfire, it was a lonely and suggestive apparition.

Tay, Muong and Thai of the north are considered culturally more advanced. Some groups are sedentary and grow wet rice and industrial crops. The tribes that practice slash-and-burn agriculture are shifting rather than nomadic in the strict sense. They may not move their village site for a generation, although their swidden agriculture forces them to change fields every year or two.

There is just enough similarity to speak of the mountain tribes in a general way. Typically, they live in small cluster villages. One exception is the dispersed tribe which believes that a mountain stream's spirit is offended if more than one family uses it. The usual village may be enclosed by some kind of bamboo fence, not only to protect against forest animals preying on the livestock, but to direct strangers to the village's single entrance and to ward off spirits coming from the wrong direction. The village and all its doors and windows may open in the direction from which the least evil might come. Early warning is afforded by clearing a no-man's land between the settlement and the encroaching forest.

The architecture varies to some degree, and there may be houses of different size and design in the same village, but they will typically be constructed on posts that raise the floor four or five feet off the ground. This gives some protection against wild animals in houses which have doorways but no doors. Privacy from visitors is achieved by pulling up the ladder or notched log that serves for steps. Often the steps will lead to an open porch across the end of the building. The interior of the house tends to stay cleaner because of this interval, especially in the rainy season. The space created beneath the house may be used as livestock quarters, children's playground, storage area, or shade from the hot midday sun. Houses are mostly built from materials at hand, although in recent years the government has urged more permanent structures of wood, masonry materials and 'tin' roofing. Bamboo is still used extensively. The roofs will be thatch from long lalang grass or other material to hand. The outside walls will be wattle.

The most common Montagnard dwelling is the longhouse, which is simply an extended house to accommodate an extended family. New segments are added at the end as the family grows. The interior is usually dark, because the roof thatch hangs low, and there may not be any windows. Near mealtime or in cool weather it will be smoky as well. The related families who inhabit the house have their own compartments, which may be separated by their individual rice bins and cooking space, but much of the living and sleeping space will be used in common.

A frequent feature inside the Montagnard house is a low platform serving as a shelf for large jars, an important part of the Montagnard culture. Rice beer is made in them, and drunk through straws during most tribal ceremonies. The ritual related to the jars is highly formalized; drinking this mild alcoholic drink, then, is anything but casual.

The way the Montagnards take a meager living from their jungle environment has undergone little change as a more complex civilization has developed in the plains. Swidden and ray are other names for the slash-and-burn agriculture practiced by the Montagnards. The farming cycle begins at the outset of the dry season with the choice of a new field for clearing. Various rites are performed to persuade the spirits to grant their consent and blessing. The trees, vines and bushes are cut and left in place to dry. The land is burned over at a time of year when the fire will not spread easily to the surrounding forest. Ash deposited by the fire furnishes needed minerals to the humus accumulated on the forest floor, which is little affected by the fire. Its natural acidity is sweetened by alkali in the ash. No other fertilizer is used, and no mechanical aids are involved in cultivation. Plowing is out of the question on land from which the roots of trees have not been removed.

At planting time, after more devout incantation, the men of the family punch holes in the ground with a 'planting stick' and the women follow behind dropping the seed and brushing dirt with their feet to fill the holes. The crop will likely be some mixture of mountain rice with pumpkin, millet, corn, squash, or manioc. The abundant rainfall, high humidity and moderate to hot temperatures of the monsoon forest guarantee conditions for rapid growth. Weeds will of course intrude, especially the second year, and the women may have to visit the field to clear them from time to time. When the new growth starts to resemble food for deer, wild pigs and birds, these intruders will have to be dealt with. More serious yet, the deer and boars may attract a tiger. If the farmer perceives the tiger as an omen signifying that the spirits are offended by the crop, he may forego the harvest from that land, however badly it is needed.

A clearing farmed in this way can produce only one or two acceptable harvests. The preparation of the next clearing is as much a part of the annual round of chores as growing the current crop. A clearing that has just been used and abandoned needs to lie fallow fifteen years or more for rotting vegetation to restore fertility to the soil. If the community using it cannot wait that long, even their first crop will be scanty.

The division of labor is as old as the culture. The men do the heaviest work involved in clearing the new fields, the carpentry of housebuilding, the metalworking, the hunting and fishing. The women do much of the work in tending the crop, and gather the products of the jungle: mint, saffron, various roots, wild fruit and berries, bamboo shoots, and other wild plants. They weave cloth and mats, cook, carry water, and tend the children. The children also pitch in as soon as they are able. They can shoo and tend the livestock, mind the younger children, and supply extra hands at harvest time, especially as gleaners. When the elderly become feeble, they can still weave mats and baskets and fashion bows and arrows. There is work for everyone.

The Montagnards hunt using spears, bow and arrow, traps and guns, and they catch fish with their own lines, traps, gigs and seines. Or they may take both game and fish with poisons that grow in the jungle and do not harm the prey as food. The hunting and fishing devices are not only effective, but beautifully made and ingenious. Museum exhibits of Montagnard crafts demonstrate both the incredible versatility of bamboo as a material and the skill of those who developed ways of working with it over the centuries. They make their own containers – baskets of every description and for every use, jars, cooking pots, and heavy wooden mortars and pestles for grinding rice into flour. Specialists in the villages are also skilled ironworkers. By bartering or selling lumber, cinnamon bark, wild honey, tea, or with money earned as wages the villagers buy iron to fashion into bush axes, sickles, machetes, hoes and other tools.

Slash-and-burn agriculture does not make for large communities. Where the slopes are steep the villages may consist of only a few families, some few dozen persons. The communities may grow a bit larger where the soil is better and movement easier. But something else is lacking for vertical growth. The tribesman's own identification is with his family and his village; his search for community does not go even as high as the tribe whose language he speaks and whose way of life he exemplifies. The notion of the 'tribe' is imposed by outsiders to define the extent of a particular combination of language and pattern of life.

The traditional ways the upland tribesmen lived in a give and take with their environment are changing now. In 1980 the resettled Vietnamese comprised a majority of the small upland population for the first time. These days some Montagnards are bringing back wages to the village from regular jobs in lumbering or on the sea, rubber or coffee plantations, or for some other work in the parts of the socialized sector that extend up into the hills. While the government has had some success in persuading villagers to settle in one place and to practice farming methods suitable to the mountain slopes they live on, it has also encountered some determined, even armed, resistance. The irony is that the resistance effort itself is bound to have a modernizing influence.

THE LOWLANDERS

The lowlands of Vietnam rise very little as one moves inland from the coast. Since the habitat of the mosquito that carries malaria in this region extends down only to 2500 feet above sea level, the line that separates the compact Vietnamese majority from the *mélange* of cultures in the hills was reinforced in a most immediate way. Lowlanders relatively free of a disease endemic in the hills would always be aware of the danger of crossing that boundary.

Lowland villages are Vietnamese villages. The line between lowland and upland and between the territories of the Viet majority and the tribal minorities is roughly the same. Exceptions are the Khmer and Cham villages that still exist in the South and the ethnic

Vietnamese who have been resettled in the Central Highlands. The Vietnamese village is a world in itself, just as the upland village is to the tribesman. Its hedge of dense bamboo has been compared to the steep ramparts of the medieval castle in Europe. But throughout recorded history it has not been the *whole* world to the villager, for it exists in a web of upward and outward relationships: the Vietnamese has long identified himself not only with his family and village, but also with his nation. This is true even in villages that represent religions different from the standard mix of Mahayana Buddhism, Confucianism and Taoism: Catholic, Cao Dai, Hoa Hao or Therevada Buddhism.

Villages differ in their configuration. In the northern and central deltas they are of course older and tend to be compact and evenly distributed over the terrain. Farmers never established separate homesteads in northern Vietnam. When the Vietnamese settled the southern deltas in recent centuries, individuals and families often claimed and cleared their own land, so that the pattern is apt to be irregular. There are separate homesteads, the villages may be strung out along watercourses or roads, and there are large farms with a central settlement. The shape of the southern village may also be irregular and discontinuous, consisting of several separate hamlets.

Houses in lowland villages are not built on stilts. The basic dwelling has a wood frame of logs, tied together at the joints in the simplest jackleg version or nicely notched, wedged and carved by a housewright. The materials used for roof and walls depend on the builder's wealth and the supply of materials. The roof may be thatch, tile or metal, and the walls may be thatch, wood or masonry, so that several combinations are possible. Regardless of the material, the floor plan is constant. On the one open side the roof forms an open lean-to. This protection shields the tenants from sun and rain while they do chores on the beaten earth in front of the doors. The interior has a dirt floor and plank beds. Woven partitions extending only up to the crossbeams of the frame serve as room dividers. The house may have an addition to one side or the other while the kitchen is attached to the rear. Lowland houses have a beaten-earth yard marked off with plants or hedge, and villagers plant gardens and fruit trees of their own.

RICE GROWING

Wet rice is the foundation on which the Vietnam village rests, though there may be regional differences in the way they grow it. In the southern delta, for instance, the planting season and rainy season begin in late April or early May. The first field task is to yoke up the water buffalo and do a shallow plowing of the seedbeds. The Khmer plow used in the southern regions is lighter than the Vietnamese plow used further north. Then several passes are made at different angles with a peg-tooth harrow, weighed down by a helper. The sprouting seed are then spread on the soft wet seedbed. Puddles are not allowed to form until the seed has rooted. From that point on the weather takes over the scheduling of operations. At a certain height the seedlings must be transplanted to the main fields, and the fast or slow onset of the rains decides when that will be. The seedlings will rot if they remain too long in the crowded seedbed.

The fields are prepared less meticulously than the seedbed. A single plowing and two passes with the harrow at right angles will do the job. Plowing with water buffalo takes five or six days per hectare and the harrowing one to three days. Tractors from the coop can speed up the work and make it easier to keep pace with the weather. When everything else is right, the calendar is consulted for a day with good portents, or at least no bad ones, and the transplanting operation is scheduled with neighbors and fellow villagers or a mutual-aid team. The transplanters start work at dawn and are fed a breakfast of rice. At eleven they break for a lunch of soup, vegetable, fish and rice, then labor on until late afternoon.

Other workers support the transplanters. Plucking the seedlings from the seedbed in bunches of 30 or 40, the worker whacks the roots against his leg to remove the mud and then binds them with cord. Another stacks the bundles in baskets and carries them suspended from a shoulder pole to the field, where he places them in the water at intervals, roots down, where the team can reach them. Keeping the plants moist in every stage is the key to success. The transplanters are also kept moist in water to their calves. Bent over, they hold a bundle of seedlings in one hand and set the plants with the other, making 'hills' of four seedlings, six to nine inches apart, in a hole they poke in the mud with the thumb or forefinger.

In the North, where rivers have to be diked, fertilizer has been indispensable for a long time. But the present high-yield rice varieties require it everywhere. As the fertilizer is applied, the stand is checked and wilting plants are replaced.

Once the crop is set, the main tasks are weeding, combatting pests and disease, and maintaining the bunds, the earth embankments that separate the fields and control the water. Weeding is a minor problem. When it is done, the women collect the plants for fodder. Once the rice reaches a height of two feet, the crop is too thick for weeds to compete. Pesticides are used against a particular green-winged insect the size of a rice kernel that attacks the leaves and stem, and against a worm that bores into the stem and causes the plant to rot.

Ample water is essential from early May to August to bring the plants almost to mature height. Breaks are made in the bunds to control the water's depth, and various means are used to lift it from canals and ditches. Until World War II a swinging scoop or basket was the only method used. Now there are pedal-power waterwheels and gasoline pumps to do the job with less labor but more expensively. The depth of the water is crucial. Much more than four inches can rot the plants; if there is much less, they may dry up.

Fields distant from the source of water are fed with the flood from the nearer fields; the stream is routed through the fields by low dikes parallel to the bunding. This is one area where collective farming is very advantageous. Optimum water use is easier to achieve by devising an overall irrigation plan and by turning the job over to a communal team than by resolving the conflicts that otherwise inevitably arise, however fairly this is done.

The mature crop is not so susceptible to peril. The tops turn a bright ocher color and give off a fragrance as they begin to bud. At this point the farmers start to drain their fields slowly so that at harvest time the soil is soft and moist, but not muddy. This helps to keep the base of the plant from rotting.

There are several harvest periods from mid-September to March, depending on the combination of crops grown and the variety of rice planted. At harvest time everyone who can goes to the fields. Once the tops have become heavy, a strong wind can tangle them, so the sooner they fall to the sickle the better. Where the sickle cuts depends on the threshing method to be used. For hand threshing the stalk must be severed close to the base. Less stalk can be taken for threshing by machine or by rolling or treading. Now the field can be left to the gleaners, mostly the elderly and children, and to the grazing buffalo.

Rice is not the exclusive crop it once was in the lowlands. Some of the former rice paddies have been given over to citrus fruit and bananas. Coconut and areca palms are sometimes planted in groves. In the latter case betel, a climbing vine in the pepper family, may be planted to twine around the palm. Corn may be combined with a crop of peas between the rows. Sweet potatoes, sugar cane, manioc and beans are secondary food crops. The house garden, fertilized with buffalo manure, ashes and leaf-straw compost, is used to grow a variety of vegetables and herbs.

Chickens, ducks and pigs forage in the farmyard, where papaya, mango, custard apple, tamarind, banana and a mixture of native fruits are planted. Some farmers may keep a buffalo or cow. Stabled at night, it roams free in the daytime and is allowed to graze in the harvested ricefield. Kapok and bamboo grow wild, but they may also be planted. The nut of the latania palm is planted along a watercourse, where in a year its fronds will grow directly from the soil to a height of 10 to 25 feet. Cut and dried, they make a good roofing material.

THE COMMUNAL SPIRIT

The village is the most constant element in Vietnamese history. It is the center of the economy and of the political, religious and social systems. A man's ties to his village are something like kinship, something born to and obtained only by birth. A man could no more 'join' another village than he could another family. There were no intermediaries between the emperor and the village in Vietnamese tradition. When a settlement became self-sufficient, the emperor would send down a name for it and name the sp[...] would ensure its peace and prosperity. His charter was place[...] sacred place in the communal building, the *dinh*, which also s[...] as meeting hall. Thus the building which the village would er[...] house the imperial charter was a physical monument to the [...] between the village and the emperor. The direct link to the emp[...] also had a ritual importance: the emperor was the sole lin[...] Heaven. Only he could perform for all Vietnamese the rite[...] propitiate the gods of Heaven and Earth. Those rites were [...] performed in 1942.

The government hierarchy, whose members foreigners cam[...] call mandarins, stood above and apart from village life befor[...] French established their administration. The village neither [...] nor wanted direction from a central government. It paid it[...] a village, but collected them by its own methods. It co[...] labor for public works, but again as a village. And it [...] for military service when that was required. Otherw[...] affairs were its own business. The saying was that [...] emperor yielded to the custom of the village.

Official authority in the village resided in [...] notables, which, like the emperor, had both secu[...] functions. The council members, men of property or l[...] real power: they arbitrated disputes, dispensed justice a[...] ment, distributed the communal grain reserve when fami[...] and allotted the communal lands among the less well-off vil[...] a kind of economic safety net. There were, then, sig[...] communal elements in Vietnamese life, more so in the North [...] the South.

Chinese patterns are evident not only in the shape o[...] Vietnamese village, but also in the Vietnamese family. There [...] couple of exceptions. The Vietnamese never took over the Ch[...] taboo against marrying someone with the same surname. Als[...] Vietnam women could own and inherit land and other property[...] preserve their property rights separate from their husband's[...] family ideal in Vietnam, as in China, is the extended family [...] when sons bring their wives into a household presided over [...] patriarch, but usually the nuclear family lives apart.

Kinship is a strong bond and follows patrilineal lines. T[...] has a ritual head, who is responsible for organizing the re[...] paid to ancestors. He may live in the house where the a[...] shrine is kept, but he will have help from other male member[...] performance of rites, just as the eldest son may inherit the [...] property housing the shrine, but otherwise is an equal heir [...] brothers. At a funeral he is the chief mourner and direc[...] proceedings. A tablet representing the deceased will be added t[...] relics on the altar. This is a society which believes that sons [...] their parents reverence and care in their old age and after dea[...] thus the perceived hardship of having no male children. Few th[...] in this world are valued as highly as continuity in the Vietnam[...] village.